Power Maths

Year 4 Practice Book 4B

Draw your favourite food.

How would you share it equally between your friends?

This book belongs to _____ .

My class is _____ .

Pearson

Contents

This looks like a good challenge!

Unit 8 – Fractions (I)

Unit 9 – Fractions (2)

Unit 10 – Decimals (I)

It's time to do some practice!

3

How to use this book

Do you remember how to use this **Practice Book**?

Use the **Textbook** first to learn how to solve this type of problem.

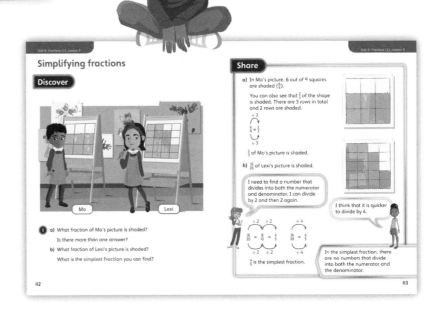

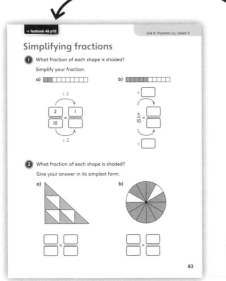

This shows you which **Textbook** page you need.

Have a go at questions by yourself using this **Practice Book**. Use what you have learnt.

Challenge questions make you think hard!

Questions with this light bulb make you think differently.

Reflect

Each lesson ends with a **Reflect** question so you can think about what you have learnt.

Reflect

How do you know when a fraction is in its simplest form?

Use **My power points** at the back of this book to keep track of what you have learnt.

My journal

At the end of a unit your teacher will ask you to fill in **My journal**.

This will help you show how much you can do now that you have finished the unit.

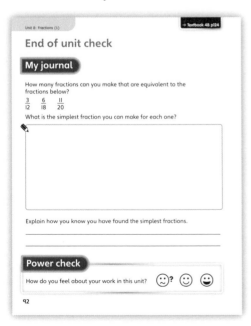

Unit 8: Fractions (1) → Textbook 4B p124

End of unit check

My journal

How many fractions can you make that are equivalent to the fractions below?

$\frac{3}{12}$ $\frac{6}{18}$ $\frac{11}{20}$

What is the simplest fraction you can make for each one?

Explain how you know you have found the simplest fractions.

Power check

How do you feel about your work in this unit?

92

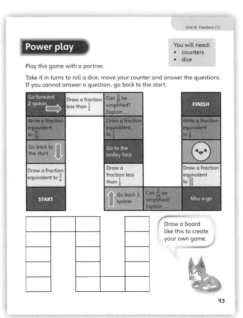

Unit 8: Fractions (1)

Power play

You will need:
• counters
• dice

Play this game with a partner.

Take it in turns to roll a dice, move your counter and answer the questions. If you cannot answer a question, go back to the start.

Draw a board like this to create your own game.

93

Problem solving – addition and multiplication

1 How many counters are there in total? Complete the two methods.

Method I: multiply first and then add.

$5 \times 4 = \boxed{}$

$5 \times 3 = \boxed{}$

$\boxed{} + \boxed{} = \boxed{}$

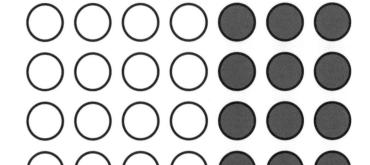

Method 2: add first and then multiply.

$\boxed{} + \boxed{} = \boxed{}$

$\boxed{} \times 5 = \boxed{}$

There are $\boxed{}$ counters in total.

2 How many pens are there in total?

$\boxed{} + \boxed{} = \boxed{}$

$\boxed{} \times \boxed{} = \boxed{}$

There are $\boxed{}$ pens in total.

3 Work out the total number of balls.

a)

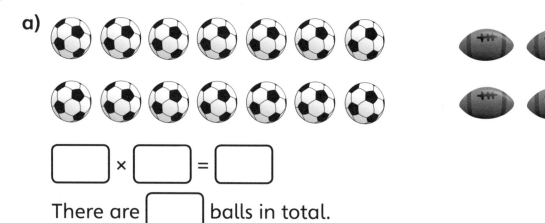

$$\boxed{} \times \boxed{} = \boxed{}$$

There are $\boxed{}$ balls in total.

b)

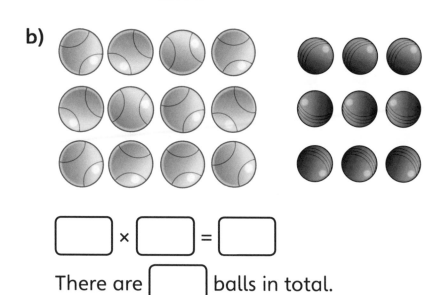

$$\boxed{} \times \boxed{} = \boxed{}$$

There are $\boxed{}$ balls in total.

4 Explain why the sum of 4×3 and 5×3 is the same as 9×3.

Use diagrams or counters to help you.

5 Complete the number sentences.

a) $4 \times 6 + 3 \times 6 = \boxed{} \times 6$

b) $7 \times 5 + 3 \times 5 = \boxed{} \times 5$

c) $9 \times 4 + \boxed{} \times 4 = 11 \times 4$

d) $5 \times 2 + 1 \times 2 = \boxed{} \times 2$

e) $4 \times 2 + 2 \times 5 = \boxed{} \times 2$

f) $\boxed{} \times 3 + 5 \times 3 = 9 \times 3$

6 Explain the method you would use to work out the total number of counters.

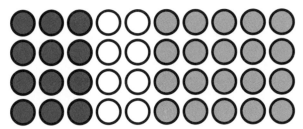

CHALLENGE

First I _____

_____.

Then I _____

_____.

There are $\boxed{}$ counters in total.

Reflect

Explain why $5 \times 3 + 2 \times 3$ is the same as 7×3.

Problem solving – mixed problems

1 **a)** Jamie has 6 packs of monster trading cards.

How many cards does she have in total?

$\boxed{} \times \boxed{} = \boxed{}$

Jamie has $\boxed{}$ cards in total.

b) Jamie shares the cards between herself and Richard.

How many cards do they each get?

$\boxed{} \div \boxed{} = \boxed{}$

Jamie and Richard each get $\boxed{}$ cards.

2 These apples are shared between 4 horses.

How many apples does each horse get?

$\boxed{} \times \boxed{} = \boxed{}$

$\boxed{} \div \boxed{} = \boxed{}$

Each horse gets $\boxed{}$ apples.

3 These towers of cubes are put into new towers of 3 cubes.

How many towers of 3 cubes can be made?

☐ towers of 3 cubes can be made.

4 Work out the missing value in each of the bar models.

a)

☐

9	9

☐		

b)

☐

12	12	12	12

☐					

5 How much does I teddy bear weigh?

I teddy bear weighs [   ] kg.

---

6 8 small ice cream cones cost the same as 6 large cones.

The small cones cost £3 each.

How much do 5 large cones cost?

CHALLENGE

Reflect

Draw a bar model to show that 2 pineapples cost the same as 5 apples.
Label the bars. Explain to a partner how your bar model shows the problem.

→ Textbook 4B p16

Using written methods to multiply

1 How many eggs are there in total?

a)

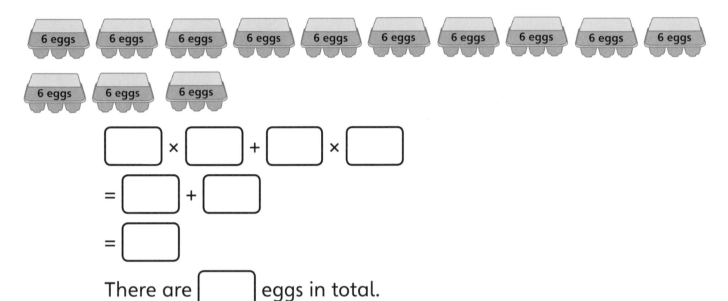

$$\boxed{} \times \boxed{} + \boxed{} \times \boxed{}$$

$$= \boxed{} + \boxed{}$$

$$= \boxed{}$$

There are $\boxed{}$ eggs in total.

b)

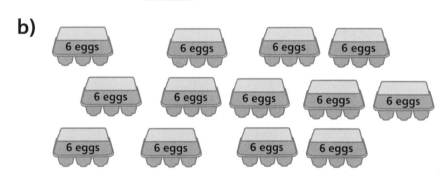

$$\boxed{} \times \boxed{} = \boxed{}$$

There are $\boxed{}$ eggs in total.

c) What do you notice about your two answers above? Why is this the case?

_____

_____

_____

2 How many beads are there in total?

$10 \times 3 = \boxed{}$

$\boxed{} + \boxed{} = \boxed{}$

There are $\boxed{}$ beads in total.

$8 \times 3 = \boxed{}$

So, $18 \times 3 = \boxed{}$

3 Complete the multiplication facts.

a) $10 \times 5 = \boxed{}$

$7 \times 5 = \boxed{}$

$17 \times 5 = \boxed{}$

b) $4 \times 10 = \boxed{}$

$4 \times 6 = \boxed{}$

$4 \times 16 = \boxed{}$

c) $3 \times 6 = \boxed{}$

$20 \times 6 = \boxed{}$

$23 \times 6 = \boxed{}$

d) $3 \times 40 = \boxed{}$

$3 \times 5 = \boxed{}$

$3 \times 45 = \boxed{}$

e) $20 \times 8 = \boxed{}$

$5 \times 8 = \boxed{}$

$25 \times 8 = \boxed{}$

f) $11 \times 7 = \boxed{}$

$5 \times 7 = \boxed{}$

$16 \times 7 = \boxed{}$

4 Complete the part-whole models.

a)

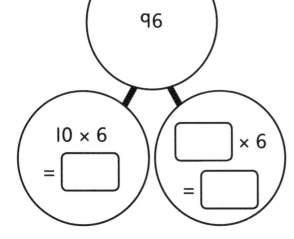

b)

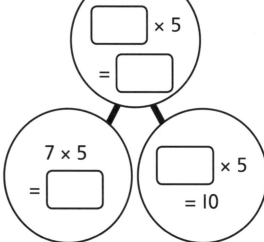

13

5 Complete the calculations.

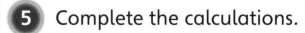

a) $8 \times 10 + 8 \times 3 = \boxed{} \times 13$

b) $9 \times 10 + 9 \times 2 = 9 \times \boxed{}$

c) $10 \times 5 + 3 \times 5 = \boxed{} \times 5$

d) $7 \times 6 + 10 \times 6 = \boxed{} \times \boxed{}$

e) $4 \times 10 + 4 \times \boxed{} = 4 \times 17$

f) $9 \times 2 + 2 \times 10 = \boxed{} \times 2$

g) $3 \times 10 + 3 \times 10 + 3 \times 5 = \boxed{} \times \boxed{}$

CHALLENGE

Reflect

Find two ways of working out the total number of pencils.

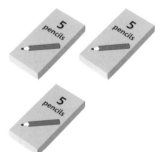

Multiplying a 2-digit number by a 1-digit number

1 The place value counters show a multiplication.

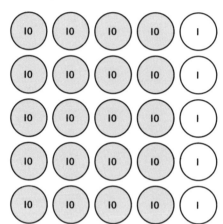

Complete the multiplication and then find the answer.

```
      4  1
×  _____
   _____
```

2 Fill in the missing numbers.

a)
```
     5  3
×       6
_____
_____
```

c)
```
     2  9
×       4
_____
_____
```

b)
```
     4  7
×       3
_____
_____
```

d)
```
     2  2
×       8
_____
_____
```

I am going to use counters to check my answers.

15

3 Work out the answers to these multiplications.

a) $28 \times 5 = \boxed{}$

c) $64 \times 9 = \boxed{}$

b) $37 \times 4 = \boxed{}$

d) $7 \times 32 = \boxed{}$

4 Each day Amal travels 54 km to and from work. How many kilometres does he travel in 5 days?

Amal travels $\boxed{}$ km in 5 days.

5 Lee has made a mistake working out 54×6.

```
      5 4
  ×       6
  ─────────
  3 0 2 4
```

Thinking about place value columns might help me to explain this mistake.

Explain the mistake Lee has made.

_____

_____

_____

6 Fill in the missing numbers.

a)
```
     5   7
  ×
  ─────────
  1       1
  ─────────
```

b)
```
          2
  ×       6
  ─────────
          8
  ─────────
```

c)
```
          7
  ×
  ─────────
      8   3
  ─────────
```

For the first one, I am going to think of a number in the 7 times-table that ends in a 1.

Reflect

Explain how this diagram matches the calculation.

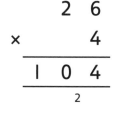

```
       2   6
  ×        4
  ─────────
   1   0   4
           2
```

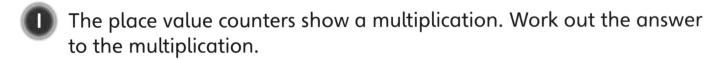
→ Textbook 4B p24

Multiplying a 3-digit number by a 1-digit number

1 The place value counters show a multiplication. Work out the answer to the multiplication.

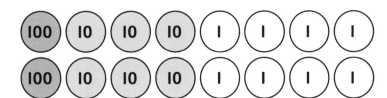

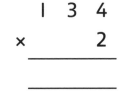

```
    1  3  4
×         2
_____
_____
```

$$\boxed{} \times \boxed{} = \boxed{}$$

2 Complete the multiplications.

a)
```
  2  1  3
×        4
_____
_____
```

d)
```
  1  4  8
×        3
_____
_____
```

b)
```
  1  1  4
×        5
_____
_____
```

e)
```
  2  5  2
×        7
_____
_____
```

c)
```
  1  1  5
×        4
_____
_____
```

f)
```
  3  1  8
×        6
_____
_____
```

3 Work out the answers to these multiplications.

a) $122 \times 6 = \boxed{}$

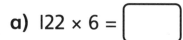

c) $270 \times 3 = \boxed{}$

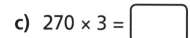

b) $215 \times 5 = \boxed{}$

d) $4 \times 624 = \boxed{}$

4 Find the missing numbers.

a)

```
      2   3
  ×       5
  ─────────
    1 4 6
          1
```

b)

```
    5 1 6
  ×
  ─────────
        1 2
```

5 A bar of soap weighs 145 g

How much do 8 of these bars weigh?

8 bars of soap weigh $\boxed{}$ g.

19

6 Alex is multiplying 136 by 7. What mistakes has she made?

	1	3	6
×			7
	7	25	3
		4	

7 Here are some digit cards.

1 **2** **5**

CHALLENGE

☐☐☐
×   7
_____
_____

☐☐☐
×   7
_____
_____

☐☐☐
×   7
_____
_____

☐☐☐
×   7
_____
_____

Arrange the number cards to make these answers:

| 1,505 | 1,064 | 3,584 | 1,757 |

Reflect

Explain to your partner how to multiply 195 by 3.

Can your partner describe a different method?

_____

_____

_____

Problem solving – multiplication

1 Emma cuts 7 pieces of ribbon. Each piece of ribbon is 23 cm long.

How much ribbon does she have?

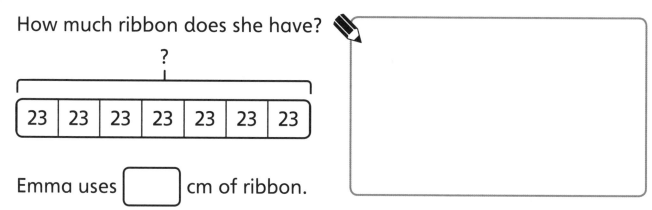

Emma uses [ ] cm of ribbon.

2 The distance from Nottingham to Lancaster is 224 km.

Holly makes this journey 3 times.

a) How many kilometres does Holly travel?

Holly travels [ ] km.

b) It costs Holly 9p per kilometre to drive her car.

How much does it cost in total for the 3 journeys?

It costs [ ] p in total for the 3 journeys.

3 Andy buys 5 bottles of juice for 79p each and 3 bottles of lemonade for £1 and 19p each.

How much does he spend in total?

| 79p | 79p | 79p | 79p | 79p | | | |

Andy spends £ [ ] and [ ] p in total.

4 A cookie weighs 67 g. There are 4 cookies in a box.

Mo buys 6 boxes of cookies.

What is the total weight of the cookies?

The total weight of the cookies is [ ] g.

5 Tower A has 7 cubes, each cube is 86 cm high.

Tower B has 4 cubes, each cube is 1 m 42 cm high.

Which tower is taller?

CHALLENGE

Remember: 1 m = 100 cm

Tower [ ] is taller.

Reflect

Explain how the bar model helps you to solve the following problem.

• Alex cycles 83 km every day of the week.

• Bella cycles 127 km every day except Saturday and Sunday.

What is the difference in the distances they cycle per week?

→ Textbook 4B p32

Multiplying more than two numbers ❶

1 What multiplication can you see in each diagram?

a)

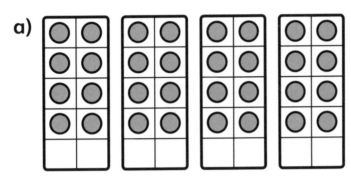

$4 \times 2 \times 4 = \boxed{}$

$\boxed{} \times 4 = \boxed{}$

b)

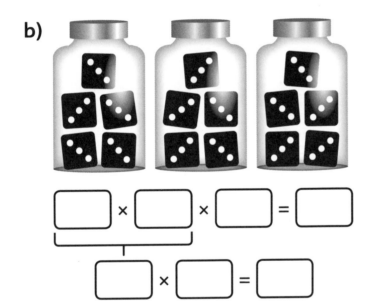

$\boxed{} \times \boxed{} \times \boxed{} = \boxed{}$

$\boxed{} \times \boxed{} = \boxed{}$

2 There are 2 boxes of chocolates. They contain 24 chocolates in total. Draw a diagram to represent what the boxes could look like.

3 Aki is working out the answer to 2 × 7 × 9.

He multiplied 7 by 9 first and then multiplied by 2.

Why do you think Aki did this?

_____

_____

_____

4 There are 11 plates with 5 cakes on each plate.

All the cakes are the same.

How many candles are there in total?

There are ☐ candles in total.

5 Work out the multiplications.

a) 2 × 4 × 6 = ☐

b) ☐ = 8 × 5 × 2

c) 4 × 5 × 5 = ☐

d) 5 × 7 × 3 = ☐

e) ☐ = 9 × 2 × 4

f) 9 × 2 × 8 = ☐

6 Fill in the missing numbers.

a) 4 × ☐ × 2 = 32

b) 2 × 7 × ☐ = 70

c) ☐ × 7 × 5 = 70

d) 54 = ☐ × 9 × 2

e) 7 × 0 × ☐ = ☐

f) 36 = 6 × ☐ × 6

7 Explain how you can work out the multiplication.

Did you use the same method as your partner?

$4 \times 5 \times 7 \times 6 \times 0 \times 3 \times 2 \times 1 = \boxed{}$

_____

_____

8 Write a number from 1 to 9 into each empty box.

How many different solutions can you find?

$\boxed{} \times \boxed{} \times \boxed{} = 216$

Reflect

How many ways can you work out $2 \times 8 \times 5$?

Which method is the most efficient?

Multiplying more than two numbers ②

1 How many beads are there in total?

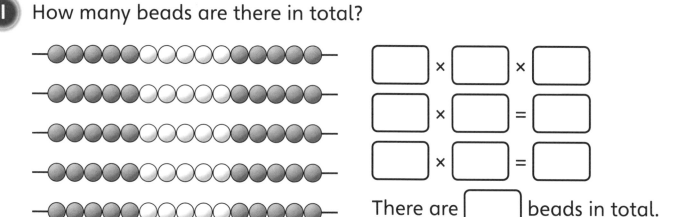

☐ × ☐ × ☐

☐ × ☐ = ☐

☐ × ☐ = ☐

There are ☐ beads in total.

2 How many counters are there in total?

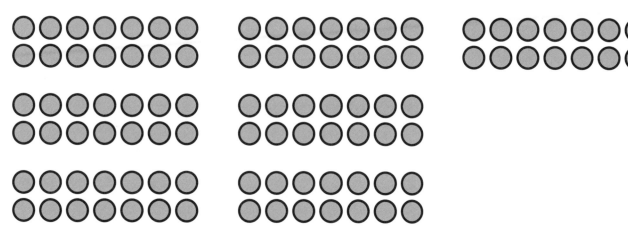

☐ × ☐ × ☐ = ☐

There are ☐ counters in total.

Explain how you worked out how many counters there are in total.

First I _____

_____ .

Then I _____

_____ .

27

3

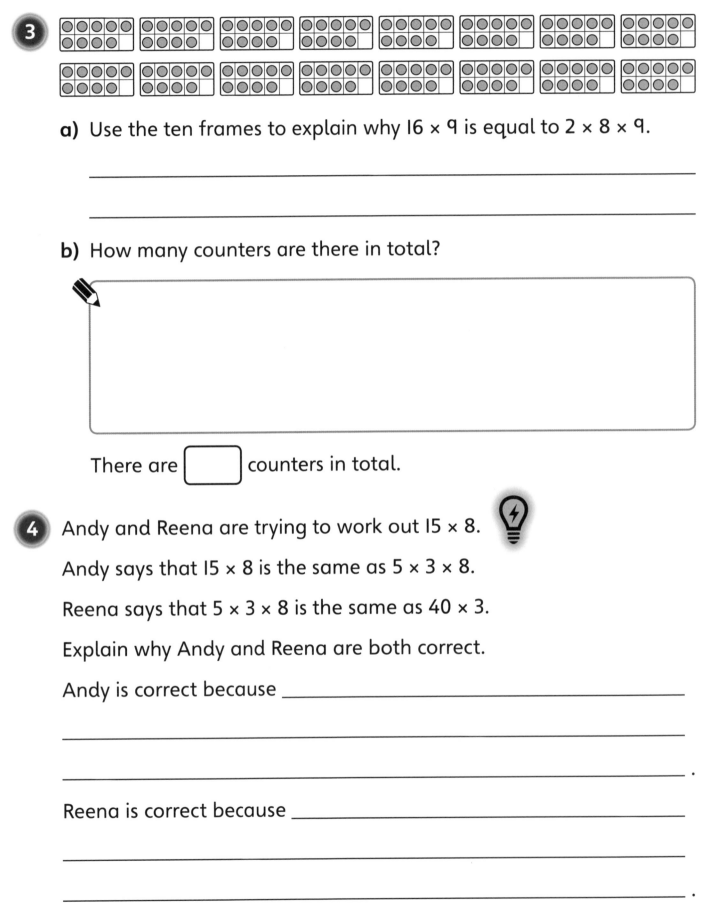

a) Use the ten frames to explain why 16×9 is equal to $2 \times 8 \times 9$.

_____

_____

b) How many counters are there in total?

There are ☐ counters in total.

4 Andy and Reena are trying to work out 15×8.

Andy says that 15×8 is the same as $5 \times 3 \times 8$.

Reena says that $5 \times 3 \times 8$ is the same as 40×3.

Explain why Andy and Reena are both correct.

Andy is correct because _____

_____

_____ .

Reena is correct because _____

_____

_____ .

5 Complete the method for working out 35 × 16.

35 is equal to 5 × ☐

16 is equal to 2 × ☐

So, I can work out 35 × 16 by _____

_____

_____ .

6 **a)** Find the answer to this calculation:

6 × 2 × 3 × 5 × 4 × 5 = ☐

b) Explain why this is the same as 12 × 15 × 20.

CHALLENGE

Reflect

Show why 3 × 4 × 6 is the same as 4 × 3 × 6.

29

→ Textbook 4B p40

Problem solving – mixed correspondence problems

a) Draw lines to show how many different ways there are to choose a bucket and a spade.

There are [ ] different ways to choose a bucket and a spade.

b) What calculation could you use to work this out?

[ ] × [ ] = [ ]

2 There are 35 different ways that Andy can choose a pair of shorts and a T-shirt.

How many T-shirts does Andy have?

[ ] × [ ] = 35

Andy has [ ] T-shirts.

30

3 Danny chooses a coin from circle A and a coin from circle B.

Write down all the possible totals of coins he could get.

A

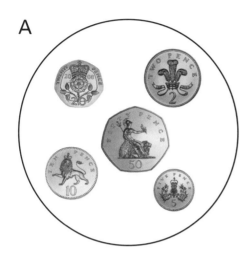

B

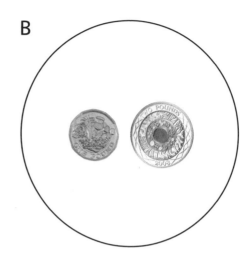

_____

_____

_____

4 Jamilla has some digit cards.

1 2 3 4 5 6

a) Show all the possible 2-digit numbers Jamilla could make.

_____

_____

_____

b) Check you have found them all by multiplying.

[ ] × [ ] = [ ]

[ ] different 2-digit numbers can be made.

5 Reena wants to buy two different snacks from the vending machine.

How many different pairs of snacks can she buy?

Reflect

How many different ways can you choose a shirt and a tie if you own 5 shirts and 3 ties?

Explain how you got your answer.

Dividing a 2-digit number by a 1-digit number ❶

1 **a)** 66 cakes are shared out equally on to 3 plates.

How many cakes will be on each plate?

66 cakes ÷ 3 plates = ☐

There are ☐ cakes on each plate.

b) What is 66 ÷ 6?

66 ÷ 6 = ☐

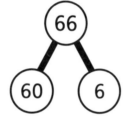

☐ ÷ ☐ = ☐   ☐ ÷ ☐ = ☐

2 Work out the answers to these divisions.

a) 64 ÷ 2 = ☐

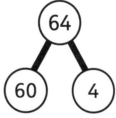

☐ ÷ ☐ = ☐   ☐ ÷ ☐ = ☐

b) 69 ÷ 3 = ☐

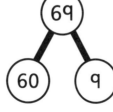

☐ ÷ ☐ = ☐   ☐ ÷ ☐ = ☐

33

3 Work out the answers to these divisions.

a) $46 \div 2 = \boxed{}$

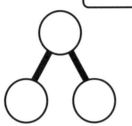

c) $77 \div 7 = \boxed{}$

b) $48 \div 4 = \boxed{}$

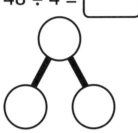

d) $93 \div 3 = \boxed{}$

4 Lexi is working out $84 \div 4$.

Can you spot Lexi's mistake?

What should she have done?

Lexi

I know that $8 \div 4 = 2$ and $4 \div 4 = 1$, so I added them together.

_____

_____

_____

5 Find the answers to these calculations.

a) $40 \div 4 = \boxed{}$

$44 \div 4 = \boxed{}$

$48 \div 4 = \boxed{}$

$52 \div 4 = \boxed{}$

b) $63 \div 3 = \boxed{}$

$66 \div 3 = \boxed{}$

$69 \div 3 = \boxed{}$

$72 \div 3 = \boxed{}$

6 Jamilla and Olivia are discussing how to solve 68 ÷ 2.

Jamilla

I know that 68 can be split into two equal groups. Half of 6 is 3 and half of 8 is 4, so the answer is 34.

Olivia

3 lots of 2 is 6, so 30 lots of 2 is 60. 4 lots of 2 is 8, so together it makes 34.

Who is correct? Explain how you know.

_____

_____

7 Explain why 48 ÷ 4 is less than 48 ÷ 2 without working anything out.

CHALLENGE

Use a calculation to check your answer.

_____

_____

Reflect

Explain how you would solve 26 ÷ 2 to someone who does not know how. Use pictures or diagrams to help.

→ Textbook 4B p48

Division with remainders

1 Use base 10 equipment to help you work out these divisions.

a) 29 ÷ 2

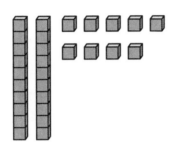

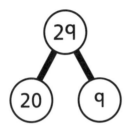

$$\boxed{} \div 2 = \boxed{}$$

$$\boxed{} \div 2 = \boxed{} \text{ remainder } \boxed{}$$

$$29 \div 2 = \boxed{} \text{ remainder } \boxed{}$$

b) 97 ÷ 3

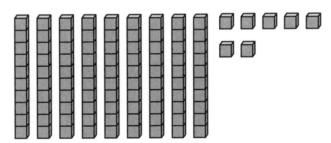

$$\boxed{} \div 3 = \boxed{}$$

$$\boxed{} \div 3 = \boxed{} \text{ remainder } \boxed{}$$

$$97 \div 3 = \boxed{} \text{ remainder } \boxed{}$$

2 What calculation is shown in the picture?

The number in the picture has [   ] tens and [   ] ones.

The picture shows [   ] ÷ [   ] = [   ] remainder [   ]

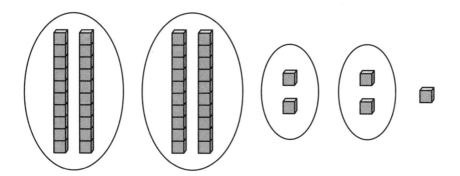

3 Find the answers to the following calculations.

a) 41 ÷ 4 = [   ] r [   ]

c) 62 ÷ 3 = [   ] r [   ]

b) 59 ÷ 5 = [   ] r [   ]

d) 89 ÷ 4 = [   ] r [   ]

4 Luis is working out the answer to 63 ÷ 2.

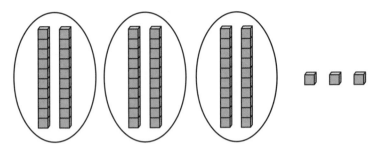

63 ÷ 2 = 20 r 3

Luis

Is Luis correct? Explain why or why not.

_____

_____

5 Using the digit cards 0 to 9, how many division calculations can you make where the answer will have a remainder of 1?

CHALLENGE

☐☐ ÷ ☐ = ☐ remainder 1

Reflect

Why is there a remainder when you divide 87 by 4? Use pictures to support your answer.

Dividing a 2-digit number by a 1-digit number ❷

1 Lexi has 38 cakes.

She shares them between herself and her friend.

How many cakes do they each get?

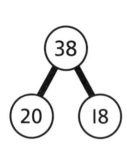

$20 \div 2 = \boxed{}$

$18 \div 2 = \boxed{}$

$\boxed{} + \boxed{} = \boxed{}$

So, $38 \div 2 = \boxed{}$

They each get $\boxed{}$ cakes.

2 Work out the following calculations.

a) $56 \div 4 = \boxed{}$

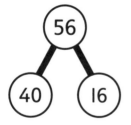

c) $96 \div 4 = \boxed{}$

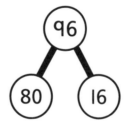

b) $45 \div 3 = \boxed{}$

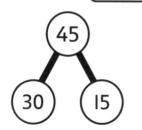

d) $76 \div 2 = \boxed{}$

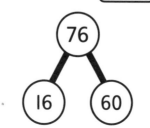

3 Partition each number to help you to work out the division.

a) $58 \div 2 =$ ☐

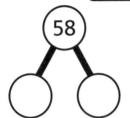

b) $65 \div 5 =$ ☐

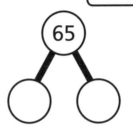

4 Find answers to the following calculations.

a) $48 \div 3 =$ ☐

c) $91 \div 7 =$ ☐

b) $92 \div 4 =$ ☐

d) $85 \div 5 =$ ☐

5 Tilly has 75 bulbs. She plants 3 bulbs in each plant pot.

How many plant pots does she need?

Tilly needs ☐ plant pots.

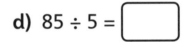
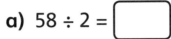

6 Which is greater,
54 ÷ 3 or 95 ÷ 5?

Show all your working.

7 What divisions could this part-whole model help you to work out?

Find three possible divisions.

48

30   18

CHALLENGE

$\boxed{} \div \boxed{} = \boxed{}$

$\boxed{} \div \boxed{} = \boxed{}$

$\boxed{} \div \boxed{} = \boxed{}$

Reflect

Does this partition help you to work out 57 ÷ 3?

What would be a better way to partition 57 to help you?

57

40   17

→ Textbook 4B p56

Dividing a 2-digit number by a 1-digit number ③

1 Lee has 3 guinea pigs.

He shares 46 dried peas between the guinea pigs.

How many peas does each guinea pig get?

How many are left over?

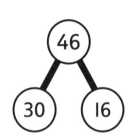

$30 \div 3 = \boxed{}$

$16 \div 3 = \boxed{}$ r $\boxed{}$

So, $46 \div 3 = \boxed{}$ r $\boxed{}$

Each guinea pig gets $\boxed{}$ peas and there are $\boxed{}$ peas left over.

2 Use the part-whole models to work out the following.

a) $67 \div 5$

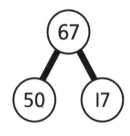

$50 \div 5 = \boxed{}$

$17 \div 5 = \boxed{}$ r $\boxed{}$

So, $67 \div 5 = \boxed{}$ r $\boxed{}$

b) $67 \div 5$

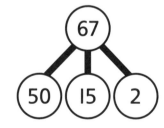

$50 \div 5 = \boxed{}$

$15 \div 5 = \boxed{}$

So, $67 \div 5 = \boxed{}$ r $\boxed{}$

3 Partition each number to help you to work out the division.

a) $47 \div 2 =$ [ ] r [ ]

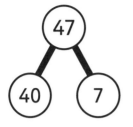

c) $50 \div 3 =$ [ ] r [ ]

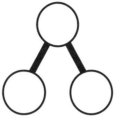

b) $79 \div 6 =$ [ ] r [ ]

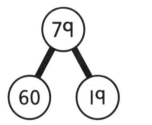

d) $72 \div 5 =$ [ ] r [ ]

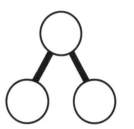

4 Work out the following calculations.

a) $67 \div 2 =$ [ ] r [ ]

b) $67 \div 3 =$ [ ] r [ ]

c) $67 \div 4 =$ [ ] r [ ]

d) $67 \div 5 =$ [ ] r [ ]

e) $67 \div 6 =$ [ ] r [ ]

5 A bar of chocolate has 5 pieces.

76 pieces of chocolate are needed to make a giant cake.

How many chocolate bars are needed?

[   ] chocolate bars are needed.

6 Danny is thinking of a number.

CHALLENGE

When you divide my number by 2 there is a remainder of 1.

When you divide my number by 3 there is no remainder.

When you divide my number by 5 there is a remainder of 1.

What could Danny's number be?
Is there more than one possible answer?

_____

_____

Reflect

How do you know that there is a remainder for 87 ÷ 4 without working it out?

What is the greatest number the remainder could be?

_____

_____

Dividing a 3-digit number by a 1-digit number

1 Work out these calculations using the part-whole models.

a) $188 \div 2$

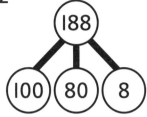

$100 \div 2 = \boxed{}$ $80 \div 2 = \boxed{}$

$8 \div 2 = \boxed{}$

$\boxed{} + \boxed{} + \boxed{} = \boxed{}$

So, $188 \div 2 = \boxed{}$

c) $195 \div 5$

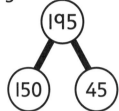

$150 \div 5 = \boxed{}$ $45 \div 5 = \boxed{}$

$\boxed{} + \boxed{} = \boxed{}$

So, $195 \div 5 = \boxed{}$

b) $189 \div 3$

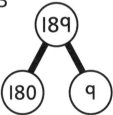

$180 \div 3 = \boxed{}$ $9 \div 3 = \boxed{}$

$\boxed{} + \boxed{} = \boxed{}$

So, $189 \div 3 = \boxed{}$

d) $275 \div 5$

$250 \div 5 = \boxed{}$ $25 \div 5 = \boxed{}$

$\boxed{} + \boxed{} = \boxed{}$

So, $275 \div 5 = \boxed{}$

2 Complete the part-whole models and then complete the divisions.

a) 128 ÷ 2 = ☐

c) 156 ÷ 3 = ☐

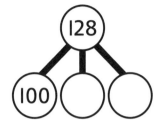

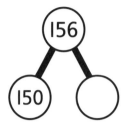

b) 128 ÷ 2 = ☐

d) 256 ÷ 4 = ☐

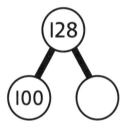

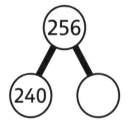

3 Find answers to the following calculations.

a) 185 ÷ 5 = ☐

c) 312 ÷ 2 = ☐

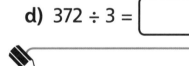

b) 264 ÷ 6 = ☐

d) 372 ÷ 3 = ☐

4 What are the division questions shown by these diagrams?

a)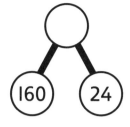

$160 \div 4 = 40$ and $24 \div 4 = 6$

☐ ÷ 4 = ☐

b)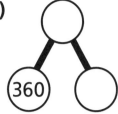

$360 \div 9 = $ ☐ and ☐ $ \div 9 = 3$

☐ $\div 9 = $ ☐

5 Show three different partitions that will help you to work out $584 \div 4$.

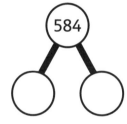

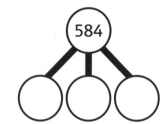

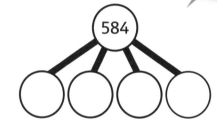

Reflect

Explain how you would work out $172 \div 4$. Why does this method work?

 → Textbook 4B p64

Problem solving – division

1 These pens are shared between 2 classes.

How many pens does each class get?

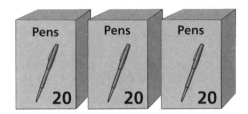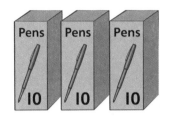

Each class gets [ ] pens.

2 Mo, Kate and Toshi share this money.

How much money do they each get?

[ ] ÷ 3 = [ ]

They each get £ [ ] .

3 44 children sing in a choir.

5 children can fit on one bench.

How many benches are needed?

⬚ benches are needed.

4 Is this sentence true or false? Circle your answer.

The remainder when 77 is divided by 2 is the same as the remainder when 49 is divided by 4.

The sentence is true / false.

5 Find three division questions with the answer 8 remainder 3.

⬚ ÷ ⬚ = 8 r 3

⬚ ÷ ⬚ = 8 r 3

⬚ ÷ ⬚ = 8 r 3

6 Some children are standing in groups of 5.

CHALLENGE

- There are 58 children.

- There are 7 groups of 5.

Can all the remaining children stand in pairs?

Explain your answer.

_____

_____

_____

_____

I can answer these questions without doing a division at the end.

Reflect

How do you know if a number divided by 5 will have a remainder?

How do you know if a number divided by 3 will have a remainder?

_____

_____

_____

End of unit check

My journal

1 Show a partner how to work out one or more of the following:

45×7 132×6 $78 \div 6$ $94 \div 5$

2 What is the same? What is different?

```
    1  2  6              1  2  6
×         3          ×         3
───────────          ───────────
    1     8          3  7  8
       6  0                ₁
    3  0  0
───────────
    3  7  8
```

Power check

How do you feel about your work in this unit?

Power puzzle

Lee is working out the remainder when 48 is divided by different numbers.

Number divided by	2	3	4	5	6	7	8
Remainder	0	0	0	3	0	6	0

Make sure you understand where each of the numbers comes from.

1 What would the table look like if Lee used 49 instead of 48?

Number divided by	2	3	4	5	6	7	8
Remainder							

2 What would the table look like if Lee now used 50?

Number divided by	2	3	4	5	6	7	8
Remainder							

3 What would the table look like if Lee used 51?

Number divided by	2	3	4	5	6	7	8
Remainder							

4 Explain any patterns that you notice.

_____

_____

_____

5 Here is another table. Work out what number Lee started with.

Number divided by	2	3	4	5	6	7	8
Remainder	1	0	3	2	3	6	3

Is there more than one answer?

Create your own table. Can your partner guess what number you started with?

Number divided by	2	3	4	5	6	7	8
Remainder							

What is area?

1 How many counters can you fit inside this square?

a) The size of the square is about

[ ] counters.

b) This is its _____ .

2 The area of these shapes has been measured in different ways.

Complete the measurements for each shape.

a) The area of this quadrilateral

is about [ ] dominoes.

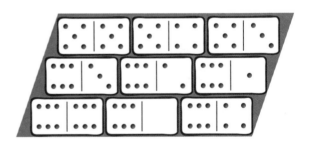

b) The area of this triangle

is about [ ] buttons.

3 **a)** Complete the following sentence.

Area is the word used to describe

_____

_____ .

b) Shade the area of these shapes.

4 Tick all of the examples that could be used to show area.

a) The number of children that can sit on a mat.

b) The number of potato prints that cover a piece of paper.

c) The number of steps it takes to walk around the outside of a field.

d) The number of bathroom tiles that cover a wall.

5 David and Sophie are measuring the area of the top of their table.

David uses playing cards. Sophie uses coins of different values.

Why has David made a better choice than Sophie?

_____

_____

6 Liam says, 'I can fit more **inside** a shape than **around** it.'

Is this always true, sometimes true or never true?

Try measuring the area of lots of different shapes to find out.

CHALLENGE

_____

_____

_____

Reflect

Find a shape in your classroom with an area of less than 15 counters.

The area of this shape is [   ] counters.

• The area can be measured by _____

• _____

• _____

Counting squares ①

① Draw lines to match each shape with its area.

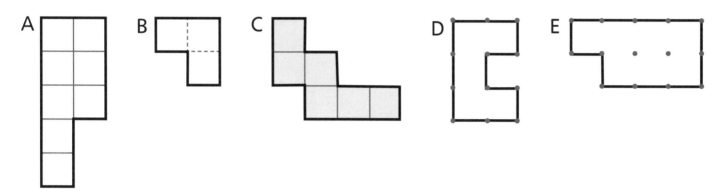

A	B	C	D	E
Area = 7 squares	Area = 6 squares	Area = 3 squares	Area = 8 squares	Area = 5 squares

② a) Complete the table below to show the areas.

Shape	Area (squares)
A	
B	
C	
D	
E	

A B C D E

b) Shapes ☐ and ☐ have the same area.

3 Georgia is measuring the area of a piece of paper. She fits exactly 2 rows of 4 squares inside the shape. What is the area of the piece of paper?

The area of the piece of paper is ☐ squares.

4 Ebo has filled this rectangle in with squares. He says this shows it has an area of 7 squares. What mistake has he made?

_____

_____

_____

5 Crack the code! Count the squares to identify the letters and it will give you the name of an object to measure the area of.

KEY: I square = A   2 squares = B   3 squares = E   4 squares = F
5 squares = L   6 squares = O   7 squares = P   8 squares = T

6 Here is a sequence of squares.

a) Write the area underneath each shape.

CHALLENGE

_____ _____ _____   _____

b) What will be the areas of the next three shapes in the sequence?

_____

_____

_____

Discuss with a partner how you can find the answers without drawing the shapes.

Reflect

Explain how you have learnt to find the area of a shape.

→ Textbook 4B p80

Counting squares ❷

1 Here is a plan of a child's bedroom.

Bookshelf

Mat

Bed

Desk

Chair

Wardrobe

a) Complete the table to show the area of each object on the plan.

b) Draw your own object on the plan and in the last line of the table write down its area.

Object	Area (squares)
Desk	
Chair	
Wardrobe	
Mat	
Bookshelf	
Bed	
_____	

2 Look at the shapes and complete the statements.

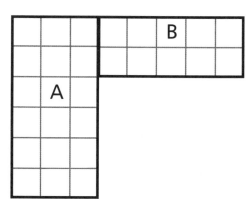

Rectangle A has an area of ☐ squares.

Rectangle B has an area of ☐ squares.

Area of A + B = ☐ squares + ☐ squares = ☐ squares

The whole shape has an area of ☐ squares.

3 A shape is made up of two rectangles joined together.

The first rectangle has twice the area of the second.

What could the total area be?

Draw your shape then work out its area.

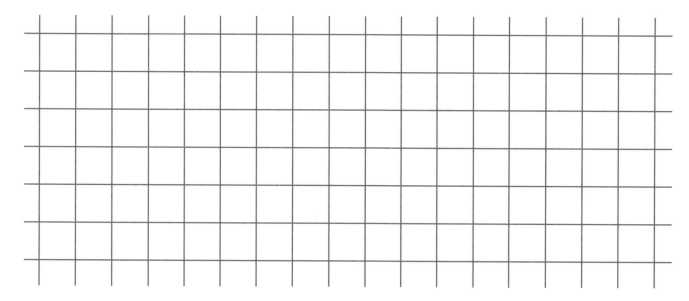

Total area = ☐ squares + ☐ squares = ☐ squares

4 What is the area of the
shaded shape?

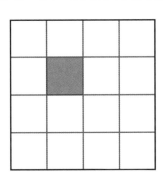

_____

5 A farmer wants to split his
land into 5 fields, all the
same area.

On the map, the grey square
shows the farmhouse and the
rest of the squares show the
area of the land around it.

Draw lines on the map to show
how he can split up his land.

MAP OF OAK FARM

CHALLENGE

I have found a way to do
this where the fields are
all the same shape, too!

Reflect

Abdul puts a cardboard shape on top of some squared paper.
How would you help him to find the area of the shape?

_____

_____

_____

_____

Making shapes

1 A builder is making a patio out of 5 square concrete slabs.

What shapes could he make?

Draw five different shapes in the space below.

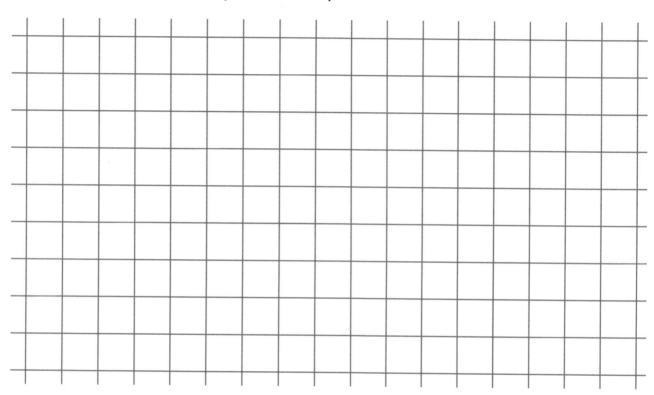

2 Draw two different rectilinear shapes each with an area of 6 squares.

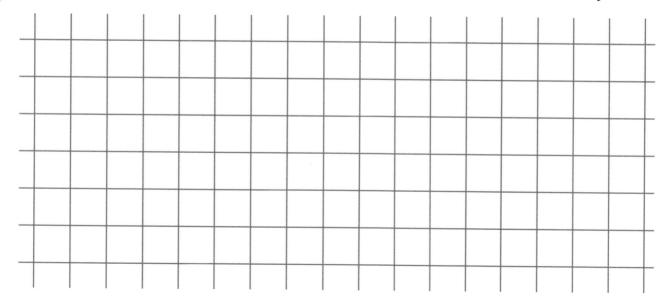

3 Tick the patios that can be made using 4 square concrete slabs.

4 Class 4 have been asked to make as many different shapes as possible using 3 squares.

They draw the following shapes.

a) What mistake have they made?

_____

_____

b) How can they make sure they do not make this mistake again?

_____

_____

5 Write your first name using squares then answer the questions below.

CHALLENGE

a) Write down the area of each letter underneath it.

b) Which letter has the largest area? Letter ☐

c) What is the total area of your name? ☐ squares

Reflect

Kyle is learning how to make different rectilinear shapes out of the same number of squares.

Write three rules to help him to know what to do.

1. _____

2. _____

3. _____

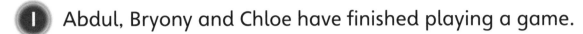 → Textbook 4B p88

Comparing area

1 Abdul, Bryony and Chloe have finished playing a game.

The winner is the person who has made the shape with the largest area.

a) Without counting, who do you think has won the game?

_____

b) Now count the squares to complete the table.

Player	Area of shape
Abdul	
Bryony	
Chloe	

Abdul

Bryony

Chloe

c) Who has won the game? Explain how you know.

_____

_____

2 Look carefully at the shapes on this board.

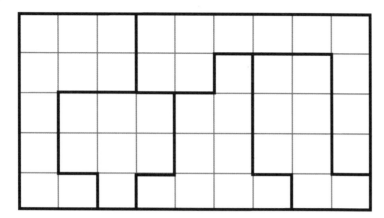

a) Label the shape with the smallest area A.

b) Label the shape with the greatest area B.

c) The area of the whole board is ☐ squares.

3 Write the area of each shape in the box underneath, then colour in the shape with the larger area in each pair.

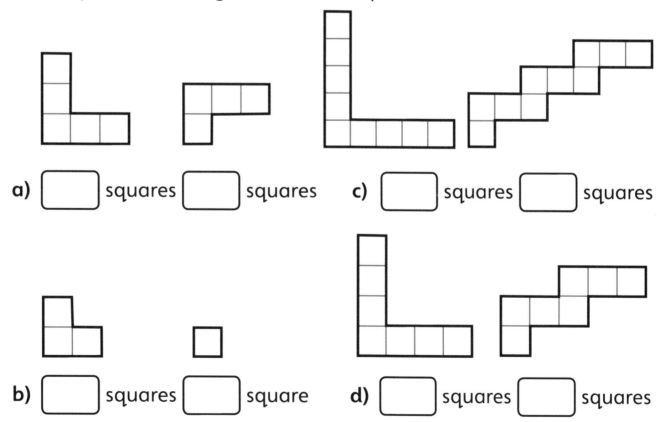

a) ☐ squares ☐ squares   c) ☐ squares ☐ squares

b) ☐ squares ☐ square   d) ☐ squares ☐ squares

4 Is it always, sometimes or never true that taller, wider shapes have a greater area than shorter, narrower shapes?

CHALLENGE

_____

_____

Draw some shapes to try out your ideas.

Reflect

To compare the areas of two shapes, I would _____

_____

_____

_____

End of unit check

My journal

Draw three different shapes, each with an area of 12 squares.

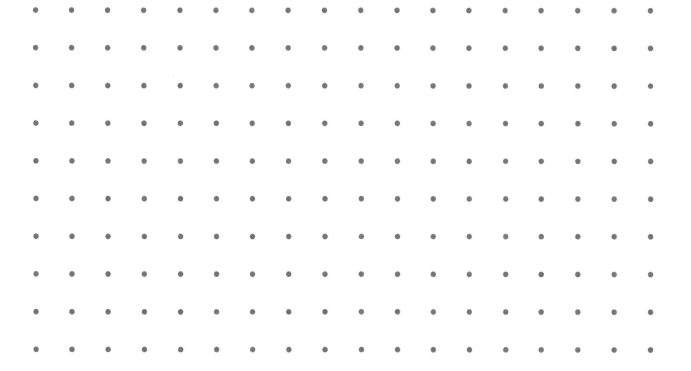

Explain how you decided the measurements for your shapes.

_____

_____

Power check

How do you feel about your work in this unit?

Power play

Aaron has dropped 2 chocolate bars on the floor.

They have broken into 8 pieces.

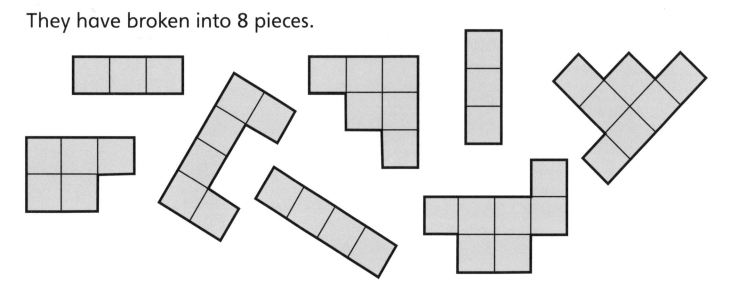

Use square dotted paper to copy and cut out each of these 8 shapes.

a) The 2 chocolate bars were both rectangles, but they had different areas. Move your shapes around to make both rectangles.

b) The areas of the chocolate bars are ⬚ squares and ⬚ squares.

c) Which bar would you choose and why? Use the word 'area' in your answer!

_____

_____

_____

Make your own puzzle by cutting up 2 rectangles. Give your partner a clue about the rectangles. Can they find their areas?

Tenths and hundredths

1 What fraction of each grid is shaded?

a)

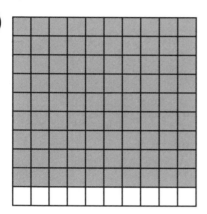

[   ] tenths are shaded.

$\dfrac{[\ ]}{10}$ are shaded.

d)

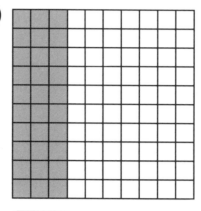

[   ] tenths are shaded.

$\dfrac{[\ ]}{[\ ]}$ are shaded.

b)

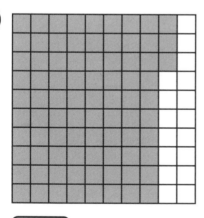

[   ] hundredths are shaded.

$\dfrac{[\ ]}{100}$ are shaded.

e)

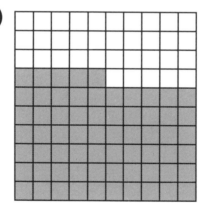

[   ] hundredths are shaded.

$\dfrac{[\ ]}{100}$ are shaded.

c)

[   ] tenths are shaded.

2 **a)** Represent $\frac{7}{10}$ on each of the grids below.

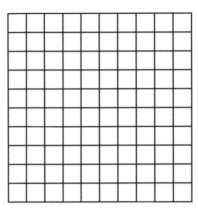

b) Show $\frac{31}{100}$ on this grid.

What fraction of your grid is not shaded?

$\boxed{}$ / $\boxed{}$ are not shaded.

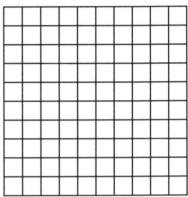

3 Andy says that $\frac{96}{100}$ of the grid is shaded.

Bella says that $\frac{9}{10} + \frac{6}{100}$ of the grid is shaded.

Emma says that $\frac{8}{10} + \frac{16}{100}$ of the grid is shaded.

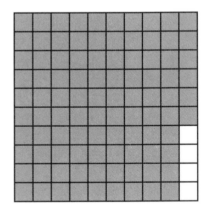

Explain why they are all correct.

_____

_____

_____

4 Work out the total shaded area in each diagram.

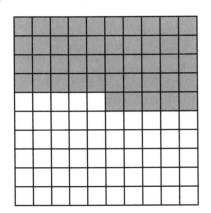

There are ☐ tenths

and ☐ hundredths.

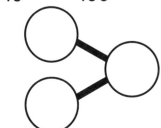

$\frac{☐}{10} + \frac{☐}{100} = \frac{☐}{100}$

There are ☐ tenths

and ☐ hundredths.

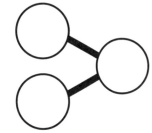

$\frac{☐}{10} + \frac{☐}{100} = \frac{☐}{100}$

Reflect

How could you find a tenth and a hundredth of a square piece of paper? Explain your answer.

Tenths and hundredths ❷

1 Complete the missing numbers.

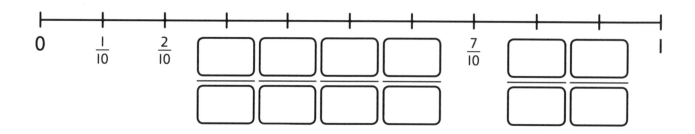

2 What fraction is shown on each number line?

a)

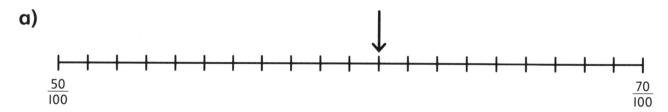

The fraction shown is ⬚ hundredths or $\dfrac{\boxed{}}{100}$.

b)

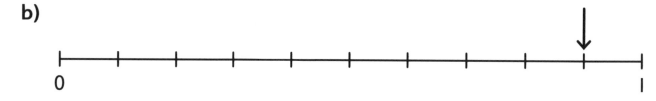

The fraction shown is ⬚ tenths or $\dfrac{\boxed{}}{10}$.

c)

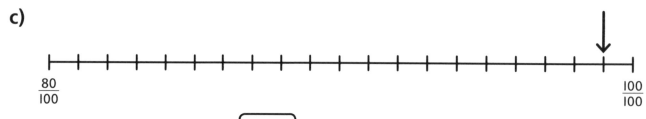

The fraction shown is $\dfrac{\boxed{}}{\boxed{}}$.

3 Use the diagrams to explain why $\frac{3}{10}$ is the same as $\frac{30}{100}$.

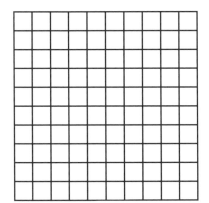 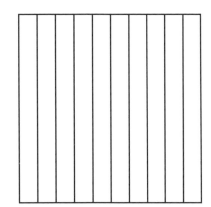

It is the same because _____

_____.

4 Complete the following.

a) $\frac{7}{10} = \dfrac{\boxed{}}{100}$

b) $\frac{5}{10} = \dfrac{\boxed{}}{100}$

c) $\dfrac{\boxed{}}{10} = \dfrac{10}{100}$

d) $\dfrac{\boxed{}}{10} = \dfrac{90}{100}$

5 Use the diagrams to help you complete the calculations.

a)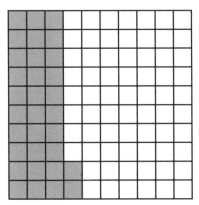

$\dfrac{32}{100} = \dfrac{\boxed{}}{10} + \dfrac{\boxed{}}{100}$

b)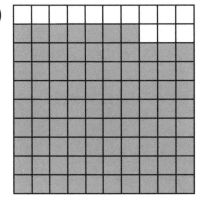

$\dfrac{87}{100} = \dfrac{\boxed{}}{10} + \dfrac{\boxed{}}{100}$

75

6 Draw an arrow from each fraction to the correct place on the number line.

CHALLENGE

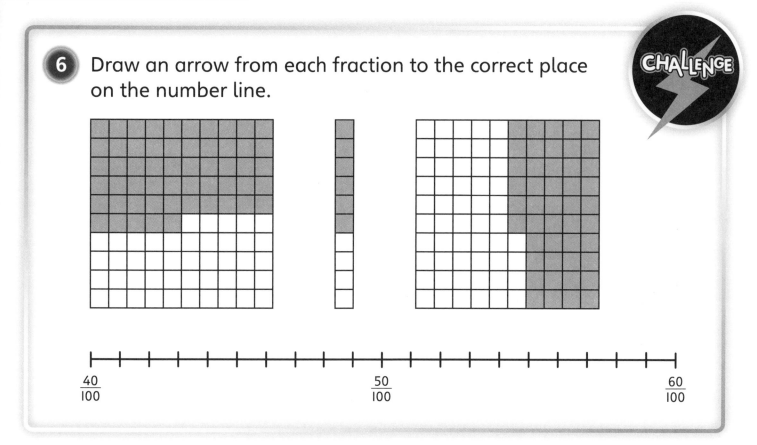

$\frac{40}{100}$ $\frac{50}{100}$ $\frac{60}{100}$

Reflect

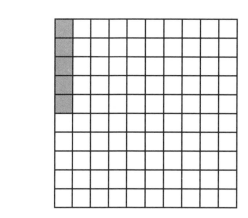

Aki thinks these two grids show the same fraction.
Do you agree? Explain your answer.

Equivalent fractions ❶

1 Shade an equivalent fraction to the fraction given.

Write down the equivalent fractions.

a)

$\frac{1}{3}$	$\frac{1}{3}$	$\frac{1}{3}$

$\frac{1}{6}$	$\frac{1}{6}$	$\frac{1}{6}$	$\frac{1}{6}$	$\frac{1}{6}$	$\frac{1}{6}$

$$\frac{2}{3} = \frac{\boxed{}}{6}$$

b)

$\frac{1}{8}$	$\frac{1}{8}$	$\frac{1}{8}$	$\frac{1}{8}$	$\frac{1}{8}$	$\frac{1}{8}$	$\frac{1}{8}$	$\frac{1}{8}$

$$\frac{\boxed{}}{\boxed{}} = \frac{\boxed{}}{\boxed{}}$$

c)

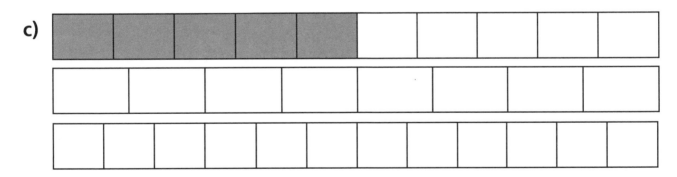

$$\frac{\boxed{}}{\boxed{}} = \frac{\boxed{}}{\boxed{}} = \frac{\boxed{}}{\boxed{}}$$

2 Use the fraction wall to say whether these fractions are equivalent or not.

a) $\frac{5}{8}$ _____ equal to $\frac{1}{2}$.

b) $\frac{3}{6}$ _____ equal to $\frac{3}{9}$.

c) $\frac{4}{8}$ _____ equal to $\frac{1}{4}$.

d) $\frac{4}{6}$ _____ equal to $\frac{6}{9}$.

e) $\frac{4}{4}$ _____ equal to $\frac{9}{9}$.

$\frac{1}{3}$		$\frac{1}{3}$		$\frac{1}{3}$	
$\frac{1}{4}$	$\frac{1}{4}$		$\frac{1}{4}$		$\frac{1}{4}$
$\frac{1}{6}$	$\frac{1}{6}$	$\frac{1}{6}$	$\frac{1}{6}$	$\frac{1}{6}$	$\frac{1}{6}$
$\frac{1}{8}$ $\frac{1}{8}$	$\frac{1}{8}$ $\frac{1}{8}$	$\frac{1}{8}$ $\frac{1}{8}$	$\frac{1}{8}$ $\frac{1}{8}$		
$\frac{1}{9}$ $\frac{1}{9}$ $\frac{1}{9}$	$\frac{1}{9}$ $\frac{1}{9}$ $\frac{1}{9}$	$\frac{1}{9}$ $\frac{1}{9}$ $\frac{1}{9}$			

3 Use the fraction strips to show that these statements are true.

a) $\frac{1}{3}$ is equal to $\frac{3}{9}$.

b) $\frac{2}{5}$ is equal to $\frac{4}{10}$.

c) $\frac{1}{4}$ is equal to $\frac{2}{8}$ which is equal to $\frac{3}{12}$.

4 Lee says that he has shown the same fraction as Zac because they have both coloured in 3 sections of their strips.

CHALLENGE

Lee   Zac

Do you agree? Explain how you know.

_____

_____

_____

Reflect

Explain how a fraction wall shows equivalent fractions.

1			
$\frac{1}{2}$		$\frac{1}{2}$	
$\frac{1}{3}$	$\frac{1}{3}$		$\frac{1}{3}$
$\frac{1}{4}$	$\frac{1}{4}$	$\frac{1}{4}$	$\frac{1}{4}$

→ Textbook 4B p108

Equivalent fractions ❷

 Use the shapes to find equivalent fractions.

a)

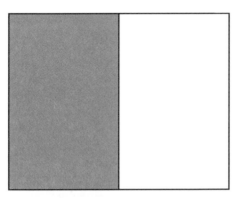

$$\frac{1}{2} = \frac{\boxed{}}{6}$$

b)

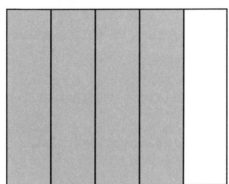

$$\frac{4}{5} = \frac{\boxed{}}{10}$$

c)

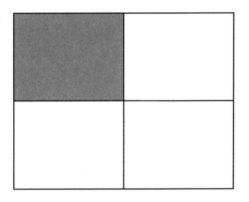

$$\frac{1}{4} = \frac{\boxed{}}{\boxed{}}$$

d)

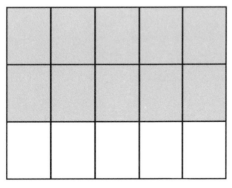

$$\frac{10}{15} = \frac{\boxed{}}{\boxed{}}$$

2 Find the missing numbers.

a) $\dfrac{1}{2} = \dfrac{\boxed{}}{8}$

d) $\dfrac{1}{6} = \dfrac{\boxed{}}{24}$

b) $\dfrac{3}{4} = \dfrac{15}{\boxed{}}$

e) $\dfrac{\boxed{}}{7} = \dfrac{6}{21}$

c) $\dfrac{3}{5} = \dfrac{9}{\boxed{}}$

f) $\dfrac{20}{24} = \dfrac{\boxed{}}{\boxed{}} = \dfrac{\boxed{}}{\boxed{}}$

3 Draw lines to connect the equivalent fractions.

$\dfrac{1}{5}$ $\dfrac{2}{3}$ $\dfrac{10}{20}$ $\dfrac{5}{6}$ $\dfrac{2}{9}$ $\dfrac{11}{12}$

$\dfrac{4}{6}$ $\dfrac{6}{27}$ $\dfrac{55}{60}$ $\dfrac{4}{20}$ $\dfrac{1}{2}$ $\dfrac{10}{12}$

4 Find numbers that can make the fractions equivalent.

a) $\dfrac{\boxed{}}{45} = \dfrac{\boxed{}}{5}$

$\dfrac{\boxed{}}{45} = \dfrac{\boxed{}}{5}$

$\dfrac{\boxed{}}{45} = \dfrac{\boxed{}}{5}$

b) $= \dfrac{6}{\boxed{}} = \dfrac{18}{\boxed{}}$

$= \dfrac{6}{\boxed{}} = \dfrac{18}{\boxed{}}$

$= \dfrac{6}{\boxed{}} = \dfrac{18}{\boxed{}}$

5 Write three equivalent fractions for each fraction.

a) $\frac{5}{6}$

b) $\frac{10}{10}$

c) $\frac{1}{8}$

6 Prove that these fractions are equivalent. Explain your reasoning to a partner.

$\frac{12}{20}$ $\frac{9}{15}$

CHALLENGE

Reflect

Explain how to find fractions that are equivalent to $\frac{1}{4}$.

Simplifying fractions

1 What fraction of each shape is shaded?

Simplify your fraction.

a)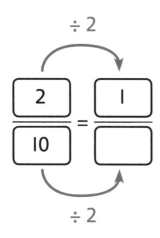

$$\frac{2}{10} = \frac{1}{\boxed{}}$$

÷ 2 (top)
÷ 2 (bottom)

b)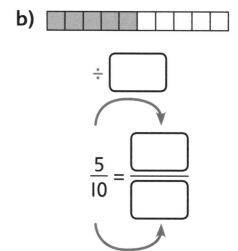

$$\frac{5}{10} = \frac{\boxed{}}{\boxed{}}$$

÷ ☐ (top)
÷ ☐ (bottom)

2 What fraction of each shape is shaded?

Give your answer in its simplest form.

a)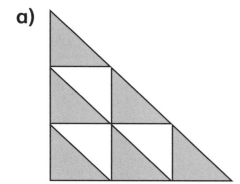

$$\frac{\boxed{}}{\boxed{}} = \frac{\boxed{}}{\boxed{}}$$

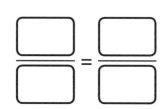

b)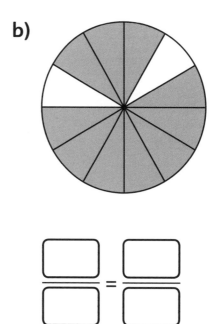

$$\frac{\boxed{}}{\boxed{}} = \frac{\boxed{}}{\boxed{}}$$

3 Draw lines to match each diagram to its fraction in its simplest form.

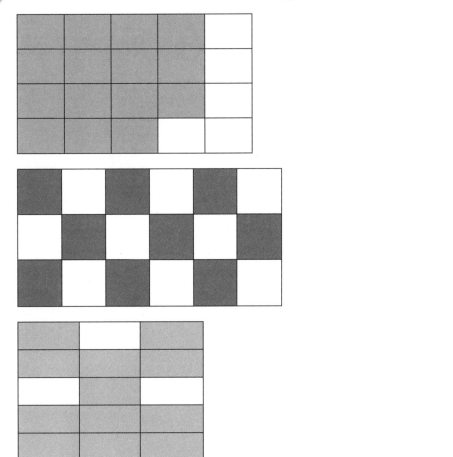

$\dfrac{2}{5}$

$\dfrac{4}{5}$

$\dfrac{1}{3}$

$\dfrac{1}{2}$

$\dfrac{3}{4}$

4 A group of friends are all given the same chocolate bar. After a week they have eaten different amounts.

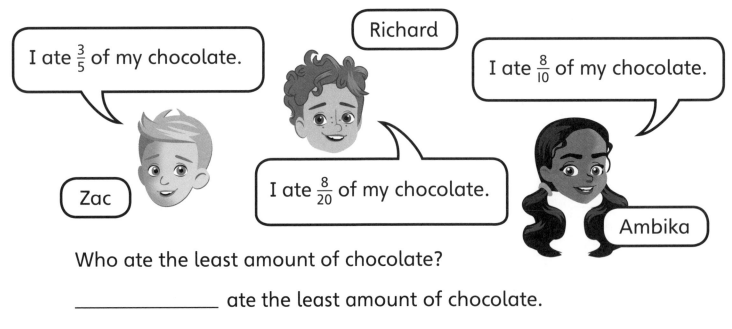

Richard

I ate $\dfrac{3}{5}$ of my chocolate.

I ate $\dfrac{8}{10}$ of my chocolate.

I ate $\dfrac{8}{20}$ of my chocolate.

Zac

Ambika

Who ate the least amount of chocolate?

_____ ate the least amount of chocolate.

5 What is the most efficient way to simplify these fractions?

a) $\frac{12}{30}$ _____

_____

b) $\frac{8}{32}$ _____

_____

c) $\frac{18}{36}$ _____

_____

6 Lee thinks that this fraction cannot be simplified any further.

Do you agree? Explain your answer.

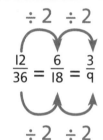

Reflect

How do you know when a fraction is in its simplest form?

_____

_____

_____

→ Textbook 4B p116

Fractions greater than 1 ①

1 **a)** Complete the part-whole model for the number of circles.

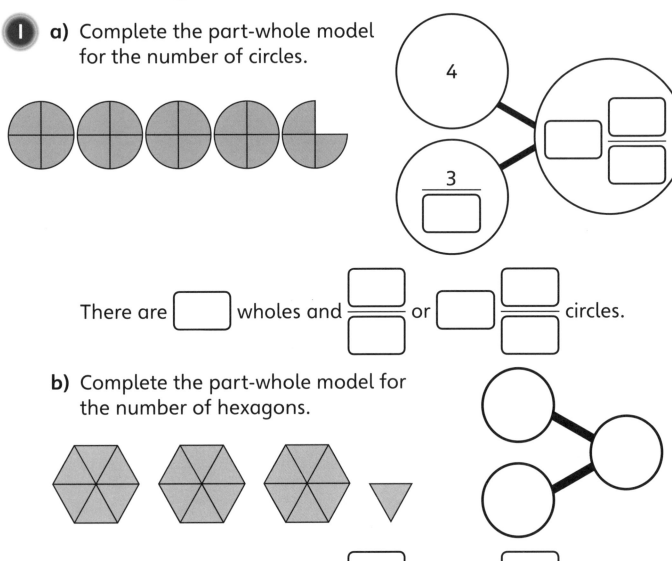

There are ⬜ wholes and ▭/▭ or ⬜ ▭/▭ circles.

b) Complete the part-whole model for the number of hexagons.

There are ⬜ wholes and ▭/▭ or ⬜ ▭/▭ hexagons.

2 Write the number of shaded rectangles as a mixed number.

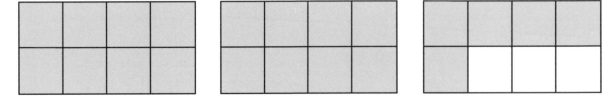

There are ⬜ wholes and ▭/▭ or ⬜ ▭/▭ rectangles shaded.

3 Shade the shapes so that they show the correct number.

a)  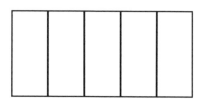 $= 1\frac{3}{5}$

b) 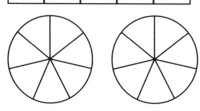 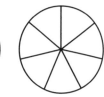 $= 3\frac{3}{7}$

4 Kate is tidying away some toy cubes.

6 cubes fit into one box.

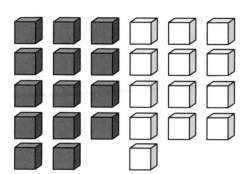

a) Kate has ☐ grey cubes.

b) Kate has ☐ full boxes of grey cubes and ☐ cubes left over.

c) Kate has ☐ ☐/☐ boxes of grey cubes.

d) Kate has ☐ white cubes.

e) Kate has ☐ full boxes of white cubes and ☐ cubes left over.

f) Kate has ☐ ☐/☐ boxes of white cubes.

5 Isla has made 4 and $\frac{3}{4}$ circles using quarter circles.

CHALLENGE

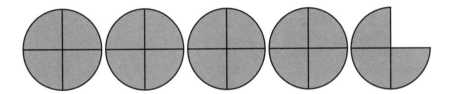

How many different ways could she complete a part-whole model to show the same total?

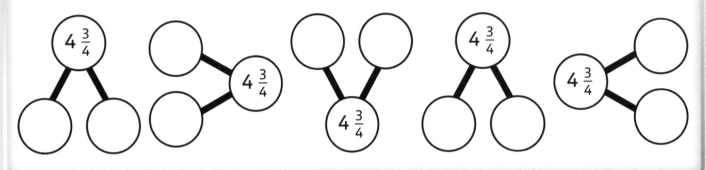

Reflect

Draw a diagram that shows $2\frac{3}{4}$.

Compare with your partner. Write down what is the same and what is different about your shapes.

Fractions greater than 1 ❷

1 Each box contains 8 apples.

13 children take an apple.

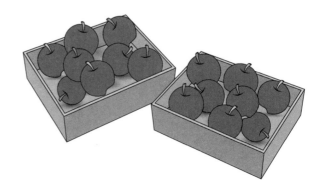

a) How many whole boxes are used?

[   ] whole box is used.

b) What fraction of a box is used?

$\dfrac{\boxed{}}{\boxed{}}$ of a box is used.

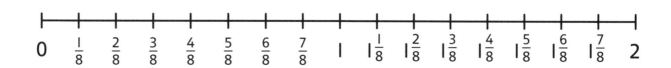

| | | | | | | | | | | | | | | | | |
|0|$\frac{1}{8}$|$\frac{2}{8}$|$\frac{3}{8}$|$\frac{4}{8}$|$\frac{5}{8}$|$\frac{6}{8}$|$\frac{7}{8}$|1|$1\frac{1}{8}$|$1\frac{2}{8}$|$1\frac{3}{8}$|$1\frac{4}{8}$|$1\frac{5}{8}$|$1\frac{6}{8}$|$1\frac{7}{8}$|2|

2 What fraction is shown on each number line?

a)

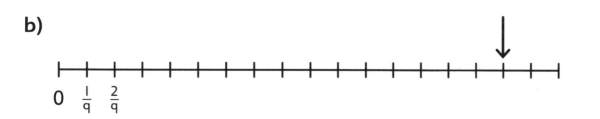

0 $\frac{1}{4}$ $\frac{2}{4}$ $\frac{3}{4}$ $\frac{4}{4}$

$\dfrac{\boxed{}}{\boxed{}}$

b)

0 $\frac{1}{9}$ $\frac{2}{9}$

$\dfrac{\boxed{}}{\boxed{}}$

3 Draw an arrow from each fraction to its place on the number line.

a) I whole and $\frac{2}{3}$ $\frac{9}{3}$ $3\frac{1}{3}$

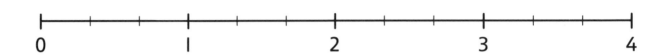

b) $1\frac{4}{6}$ $\frac{10}{6}$ 2 wholes and $\frac{5}{6}$

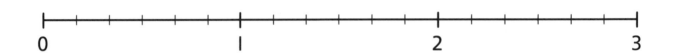

4 Complete these number sentences.

a) 2 wholes and $\frac{2}{5} = \dfrac{\boxed{}}{5}$

b) $\frac{9}{6} = \boxed{}$ whole and $\dfrac{\boxed{}}{6} = \boxed{}\dfrac{\boxed{}}{\boxed{}}$

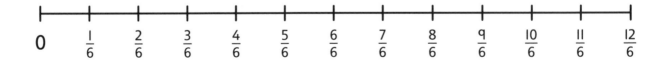

5 Write the number marked in two different ways.

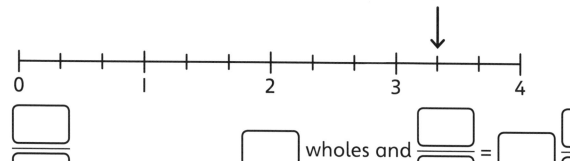

0   1   2   3   4

$$\frac{}{}$$

$\boxed{}$ wholes and $\frac{}{}$ = $\boxed{}$ $\frac{}{}$

6 Lexi draws this number line.

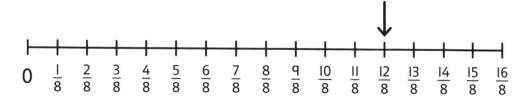

$0 \quad \frac{1}{8} \quad \frac{2}{8} \quad \frac{3}{8} \quad \frac{4}{8} \quad \frac{5}{8} \quad \frac{6}{8} \quad \frac{7}{8} \quad \frac{8}{8} \quad \frac{9}{8} \quad \frac{10}{8} \quad \frac{11}{8} \quad \frac{12}{8} \quad \frac{13}{8} \quad \frac{14}{8} \quad \frac{15}{8} \quad \frac{16}{8}$

Andy says: 'The arrow is pointing to $1\frac{1}{2}$.'

Do you agree? Explain your reasoning.

_____

_____

Reflect

Explain to a partner two different ways that fractions greater than 1 can be written.

Which way do you prefer? Explain why.

_____

_____

→ Textbook 4B p124

End of unit check

My journal

How many fractions can you make that are equivalent to the fractions below?

$\dfrac{3}{12}$ $\dfrac{6}{18}$ $\dfrac{11}{20}$

What is the simplest fraction you can make for each one?

Explain how you know you have found the simplest fractions.

_____

_____

Power check

How do you feel about your work in this unit?

Power play

You will need:
- counters
- dice

Play this game with a partner.

Take it in turns to roll a dice, move your counter and answer the questions. If you cannot answer a question, go back to the start.

Go forward 2 spaces →→	Draw a fraction less than $\frac{1}{2}$	Can $\frac{11}{13}$ be simplified? Explain ...		**FINISH**
Write a fraction equivalent to $\frac{15}{20}$		Draw a fraction equivalent to $\frac{1}{3}$		Write a fraction equivalent to $\frac{1}{9}$
Go back to the start ⬇		Go to the smiley face		😊
Draw a fraction equivalent to $\frac{3}{4}$		Draw a fraction less than $\frac{1}{3}$		Draw a fraction equivalent to $\frac{22}{33}$
START		⬆ Go back 3 spaces	Can $\frac{21}{24}$ be simplified? Explain ...	Miss a go

Draw a board like this to create your own game.

93

→ Textbook 4B p128

Adding fractions

1 Tino the horse eats $\frac{4}{5}$ of a bale of hay on Monday. He eats $\frac{2}{5}$ of a bale of hay on Tuesday.

What fraction does Tino eat altogether?

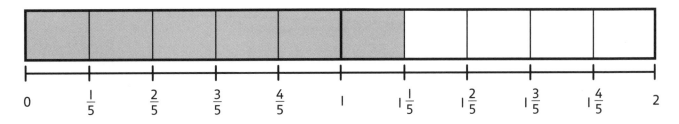

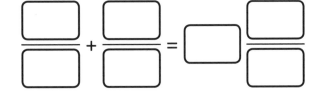

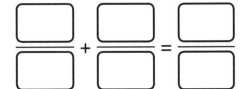

Tino eats ☐ ☐ bales of hay.

2 Alexis runs $\frac{7}{9}$ km, she has a rest and then runs a further $\frac{5}{9}$ km.

How far does Alexis run in total?

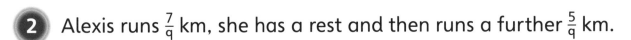

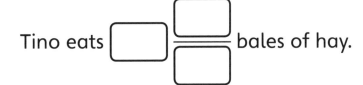

Alexis runs ☐ km in total.

3 Work out the following calculations.

Give your answers as improper fractions.

> I could draw a fraction strip to help me.

a) $\dfrac{3}{4} + \dfrac{3}{4} = \dfrac{\boxed{}}{\boxed{}}$

d) $\dfrac{3}{10} + \dfrac{1}{10} + \dfrac{9}{10} = \dfrac{\boxed{}}{\boxed{}}$

b) $\dfrac{2}{5} + \dfrac{4}{5} = \dfrac{\boxed{}}{\boxed{}}$

e) $\dfrac{3}{5} + \dfrac{3}{5} + \dfrac{3}{5} = \boxed{}$

c) $\dfrac{\boxed{}}{\boxed{}} = \dfrac{5}{12} + \dfrac{11}{12}$

f) 8 ninths + 5 ninths = $\dfrac{\boxed{}}{\boxed{}}$

4 Match the calculation to the correct answer.

$\dfrac{6}{7} + \dfrac{3}{7}$ $\qquad\qquad\qquad\qquad$ $\dfrac{11}{7}$

$\dfrac{5}{7} + \dfrac{1}{7} + \dfrac{6}{7}$ $\qquad\qquad\qquad$ 1

$\dfrac{3}{7} + \dfrac{4}{7}$ $\qquad\qquad\qquad\qquad$ $1\dfrac{2}{7}$

$\dfrac{6}{7} + \dfrac{5}{7}$ $\qquad\qquad\qquad\qquad$ $\dfrac{12}{7}$

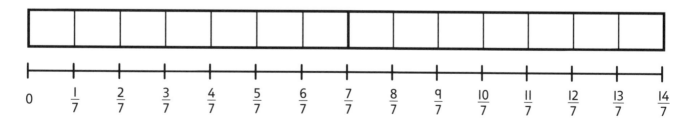

5 Fred works out this calculation:

$$\frac{3}{8} + \frac{7}{8} = \frac{10}{16}$$

a) What mistake has Fred made? _____

b) What is the correct answer? _____

6 Find the missing numbers by completing the calculations.

a) $\frac{4}{5} + \dfrac{\boxed{}}{5} = \frac{7}{5}$ $\frac{4}{5} + \dfrac{\boxed{}}{5} = 1\frac{2}{5}$ $\frac{4}{5} + \dfrac{\boxed{}}{5} = 1\frac{3}{5}$

b) $\frac{11}{13} + \dfrac{\boxed{}}{13} = \frac{17}{13}$ $\frac{7}{8} + \dfrac{\boxed{}}{8} = 1\frac{3}{8}$ $\dfrac{\boxed{}}{6} + \frac{1}{6} = 1$

c) $\frac{15}{8} = \frac{3}{8} + \dfrac{\boxed{}}{8} + \dfrac{\boxed{}}{8}$ $\frac{15}{8} = \frac{4}{8} + \dfrac{\boxed{}}{8} + \dfrac{\boxed{}}{8}$

$\frac{15}{8} = \frac{5}{8} + \dfrac{\boxed{}}{8} + \dfrac{\boxed{}}{8}$ $\frac{15}{8} = \frac{6}{8} + \dfrac{\boxed{}}{8} + \dfrac{\boxed{}}{8}$

Reflect

Draw a diagram to show that $\frac{4}{5} + \frac{4}{5} = \frac{8}{5}$.

Subtracting fractions ❶

1 Last week Rusty the dog ate $2\frac{7}{10}$ kg of dog food. This week he ate $\frac{9}{10}$ kg less than last week.

How much dog food did Rusty eat this week?

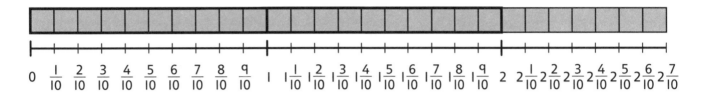

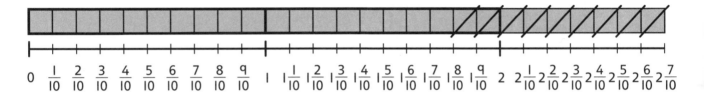

$2\frac{7}{10} - \dfrac{\boxed{}}{\boxed{}} = \boxed{}$

Rusty ate $\boxed{}$ kg this week.

2 Cross out part of the fraction strip to help you work out the answer to $3\frac{1}{5} - \frac{4}{5}$.

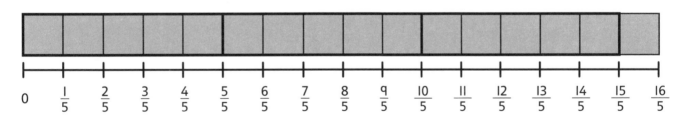

$3\frac{1}{5} - \frac{4}{5} = \boxed{}$

3 Complete each calculation.

a) $1\frac{7}{8} - \frac{3}{8} = $ ⬚

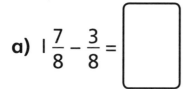

b) ⬚ $= 3\frac{1}{9} - \frac{5}{9}$

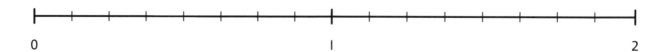

c) $2\frac{9}{11} - \frac{3}{11} - \frac{9}{11} = $ ⬚

I will do the subtractions in a different order to make this easier to work out.

4 Millie has $2\frac{5}{7}$ litres of juice. Each day Millie drinks $\frac{6}{7}$ of a litre of juice.

a) How many days will the juice last?

Millie has enough juice for ⬚ days.

b) How much juice is left over?

There is ⬚ of a litre of juice left over.

5 Work out these calculations.

a) $2\frac{2}{5} - \frac{4}{5} = \boxed{}$

d) $3\frac{2}{8} - \frac{5}{8} = \boxed{}$

g) $\boxed{}\frac{1}{6} - \frac{\boxed{}}{6} = 2$

b) $3\frac{1}{3} - \frac{2}{3} = \boxed{}$

e) $7\frac{5}{12} - \frac{11}{12} = \boxed{}$

h) $\boxed{} - \frac{7}{10} = 3\frac{5}{10}$

c) $1\frac{5}{8} - \frac{7}{8} = \boxed{}$

f) $\boxed{}\frac{1}{8} - \frac{5}{8} = 4\frac{\boxed{}}{8}$

i) $7\frac{1}{5} - \boxed{} = 6\frac{3}{5}$

6 Here are three lengths of ribbon.

Preeti cuts $\frac{7}{9}$ m of ribbon from her piece and then a further $\frac{4}{9}$ m from it.

She has 3 m of ribbon left.

Which ribbon did Preeti have to start with?

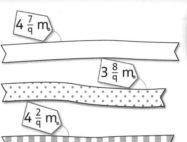

CHALLENGE

Reflect

Draw a diagram to help you explain the answer to $2\frac{1}{5} - \frac{3}{5}$.

→ Textbook 4B p136

Subtracting fractions ❷

1 Amelia has 2 cakes. She eats $\frac{3}{8}$ of one of the cakes with her friend.

How much cake does she have left?

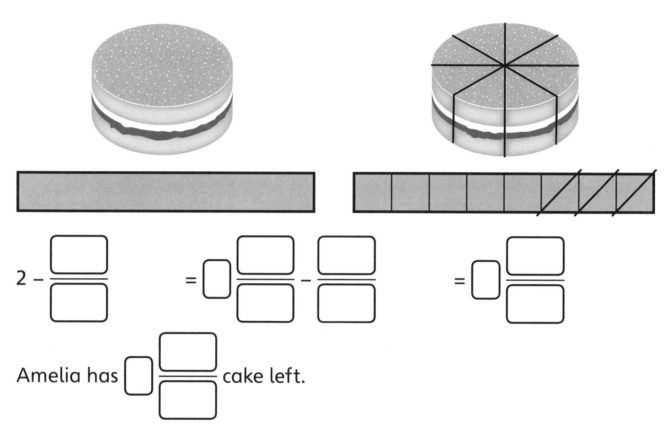

$2 - \dfrac{\boxed{}}{\boxed{}} \quad = \boxed{}\dfrac{\boxed{}}{\boxed{}} - \dfrac{\boxed{}}{\boxed{}} \quad = \boxed{}\dfrac{\boxed{}}{\boxed{}}$

Amelia has $\boxed{}\dfrac{\boxed{}}{\boxed{}}$ cake left.

2 Complete the following calculations. Use the fraction strips to help you.

a) $3 - \dfrac{1}{5} = \boxed{}\dfrac{\boxed{}}{\boxed{}}$

d) $3 - \dfrac{4}{5} = \boxed{}\dfrac{\boxed{}}{\boxed{}}$

b) $3 - \dfrac{2}{5} = \boxed{}\dfrac{\boxed{}}{\boxed{}}$

e) $3 - \dfrac{5}{5} = \boxed{}\dfrac{\boxed{}}{\boxed{}}$

c) $3 - \dfrac{3}{5} = \boxed{}\dfrac{\boxed{}}{\boxed{}}$

3 **a)** What is $3 - \frac{4}{7}$?

$3 - \frac{4}{7} =$ ☐

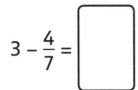

b) Mary says that $5 - \frac{2}{7} = \frac{3}{7}$.

What mistake has Mary made? Explain what the correct answer should be.

_____

_____

_____

4 Work out the following calculations.

a) $4 - \frac{6}{9} =$ ☐ $4 - \frac{7}{9} =$ ☐ $4 - \frac{8}{9} =$ ☐

b) $5 - \frac{6}{9} =$ ☐ $5 - \frac{7}{9} =$ ☐ $5 - \frac{8}{9} =$ ☐

c) $10 - \frac{2}{3} =$ ☐ $8 - \frac{2}{3} =$ ☐ $6 - \frac{2}{3} =$ ☐

d) $6 - \frac{3}{4} =$ ☐ $6 - \frac{4}{5} =$ ☐ $6 - \frac{9}{10} =$ ☐

5 Complete the calculations.

a) $5 - \boxed{} = 4\frac{3}{7}$

b) $1 - \boxed{} = \frac{1}{3}$

c) $16 - \frac{2}{9} = \boxed{}$

d) $10 - \boxed{} = 9\frac{1}{3}$

e) $\boxed{} - \frac{2}{5} = 4\frac{3}{5}$

f) $\boxed{} - \frac{1}{4} = 9\frac{3}{4}$

6 Jen is going to run 5 km. She runs $\frac{5}{8}$ km every 10 minutes.

Will she complete the run in less than 1 hour?

CHALLENGE

I remember that there are 60 minutes in 1 hour.

Reflect

Is this calculation correct? Draw diagrams to explain your reasoning.

$4 - \frac{3}{4} = \frac{1}{4}$

Problem solving – adding and subtracting fractions

1 There is 3 kg of flour in a cupboard.

a) Holly uses $\frac{5}{7}$ kg to make bread. How much flour is left in the cupboard?

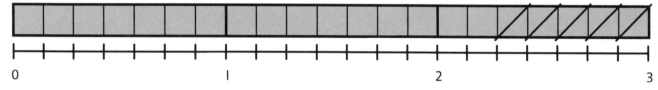

$$3 - \frac{\square}{\square} = \boxed{} \frac{\square}{\square} - \frac{\square}{\square} = \boxed{} \frac{\square}{\square}$$

There is $\boxed{} \dfrac{\square}{\square}$ kg of flour left in the cupboard.

b) Tulpesh uses $\frac{6}{7}$ kg more flour than Holly to make bread. How much flour does Tulpesh use?

$$\frac{\square}{\square} + \frac{\square}{\square} = \frac{\square}{\square}$$

Tulpesh uses $\boxed{}$ kg of flour.

c) How much flour is used by Holly and Tulpesh in total?

$\boxed{}$ kg of flour is used in total.

2 A farmer ploughed $\frac{5}{7}$ of an acre of his field in the morning and $\frac{4}{7}$ of an acre in the afternoon.

An acre is a measure of land.

morning

afternoon

How much of his field did the farmer plough in total?

The farmer ploughed [ ] acres of his field in total.

3 Abigail, Phoebe and Naomi have a bottle of juice.

Abigail drinks $\frac{3}{17}$ of the bottle.

Phoebe drinks $\frac{2}{17}$ more than Abigail.

What fraction of the juice is remaining for Naomi?

First, I am going to find out how much Phoebe drinks and then how much Abigail and Phoebe drink altogether.

[ ] of the juice is remaining.

4 Fill in the empty boxes.

$$\frac{\boxed{}}{8} + \frac{\boxed{}}{8} - \frac{\boxed{}}{8} = \frac{7}{8}$$

I can see three different ways! I wonder if there are more.

How many ways can you find to complete it?

5 Axel picked $\frac{1}{3}$ kg of strawberries and Catherine picked $\frac{2}{3}$ kg of strawberries.

CHALLENGE

Esme ate $\frac{3}{7}$ kg of the strawberries collected. What amount of strawberries were left?

$\boxed{}$ kg of strawberries were left.

Reflect

Write a story where adding or subtracting gives an answer of $\frac{4}{9}$.

→ **Textbook 4B p144**

Problem solving – adding and subtracting fractions ❷

1 Mo and Amelia each eat some Spanish omelette.

Mo eats $\frac{5}{8}$ of his Spanish omelette.

Amelia eats $\frac{7}{8}$ of her Spanish omelette.

What fraction has been eaten in total?

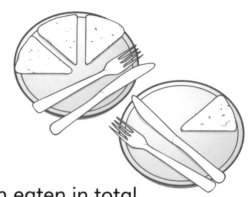

$\dfrac{\boxed{}}{\boxed{}}$ of the Spanish omelettes have been eaten in total.

2 The answer to each of the following questions is $\frac{7}{5}$.

Complete the questions.

a) $\frac{9}{5} - \frac{\boxed{}}{5} = \frac{7}{5}$

e) $\frac{10}{5} - \frac{\boxed{}}{5} = \frac{7}{5}$

b) $\frac{3}{5} + \frac{\boxed{}}{5} = \frac{7}{5}$

f) $2 - \frac{\boxed{}}{5} = \frac{7}{5}$

c) $\frac{1}{5} + \frac{1}{5} + \frac{\boxed{}}{5} = \frac{7}{5}$

g) $2 - \frac{1}{5} - \frac{\boxed{}}{5} = \frac{7}{5}$

d) $1 + \frac{\boxed{}}{5} = \frac{7}{5}$

h) $\frac{\boxed{}}{5} + \frac{\boxed{}}{5} + \frac{\boxed{}}{5} = \frac{7}{5}$

I can see more than one answer to h). I wonder how many correct answers there are.

3 Use the number lines to help you complete the following calculations.

a) $\dfrac{5}{6} + \dfrac{3}{6} - \dfrac{4}{6} = \dfrac{\boxed{}}{6}$

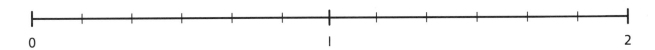

0   1   2

b) $\dfrac{7}{9} - \dfrac{5}{9} + \dfrac{8}{9} = \dfrac{\boxed{}}{9}$

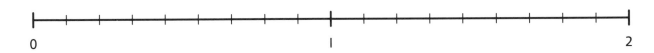

0   1   2

c) $1 + \dfrac{3}{5} + \dfrac{2}{5} - \dfrac{8}{5} = \dfrac{\boxed{}}{5}$

0   1   2   3

4 Three jars contain $\dfrac{3}{8}$ kg, $\dfrac{7}{8}$ kg and $\dfrac{7}{8}$ kg of coffee.

Each jar can hold a total of 1 kg.

How many full jars of coffee can be made using the coffee?

Explain your answer.

_____

_____

_____

_____

5 Florence and Kofi are running a race.

Florence runs 3 km in total. Kofi runs $\frac{3}{4}$ km in total.

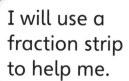

I will use a fraction strip to help me.

How much further does Florence run than Kofi?
Give your answer as a mixed number.

Florence runs ☐ km more than Kofi.

6 Work out the following calculations.

CHALLENGE

a) $\frac{3}{6} + \frac{2}{5} + \frac{3}{6} + \frac{3}{5} = $ ☐

b) $\frac{4}{7} + \frac{3}{8} + \frac{5}{8} + \frac{3}{7} = $ ☐

c) $\frac{4}{5} + \frac{1}{5} - \frac{2}{3} = $ ☐

Reflect

The answer is $\frac{17}{10}$. What was the question?

Create your own calculation.

Calculating fractions of a quantity

1 Emily has three different-sized teddy bears – a small teddy bear, a medium teddy bear and a large teddy bear.

The large teddy bear is 42 cm tall.

a) The small teddy bear is $\frac{1}{7}$ the height of the large teddy bear.

How tall is the small teddy bear?

$$\boxed{} \div \boxed{} = \boxed{}$$

42 cm

? cm

The small teddy bear is $\boxed{}$ cm tall.

b) The medium teddy bear is $\frac{4}{7}$ the height of the large teddy bear.

How tall is the medium teddy bear?

$$\boxed{} \div \boxed{} = \boxed{}$$
$$\boxed{} \times \boxed{} = \boxed{}$$

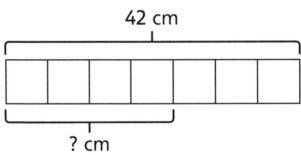

42 cm

? cm

The medium teddy bear is $\boxed{}$ cm tall.

2 Complete each question.

a) $\frac{1}{3}$ of 30 m = ☐ m

b) $\frac{2}{3}$ of 27 kg = ☐ kg

c) $\frac{5}{6}$ of £18 = £☐

3 Is this statement true or false?

$\frac{3}{8}$ of 24 = $\frac{1}{4}$ of 36

Show your working out and circle your answer.

4 Match each calculation to the correct answer.

$\frac{2}{3}$ of 18   15

$\frac{1}{9}$ of 18   7

$\frac{5}{6}$ of 18   2

$\frac{7}{18}$ of 18   12

5 Complete the following calculations.

a) $\frac{1}{3}$ of $\boxed{}$ = 2

c) $\frac{1}{\boxed{}}$ of 70 kg = 10 kg

b) $\frac{1}{5}$ of $\boxed{}$ = 8

d) $\frac{\boxed{}}{\boxed{}}$ of 42 = 35

6 Chloe got $\frac{5}{7}$ of her test correct.

Mike got $\frac{3}{8}$ of the same test incorrect.

The test was out of 56 marks.

Who got more marks and by how many?

CHALLENGE

Reflect

Write a question that could go with this diagram.

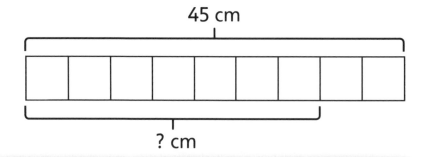

45 cm

? cm

→ Textbook 4B p152

Problem solving – fraction of a quantity ❶

1 **a)** Amelia has completed $\frac{1}{6}$ of her maths homework.

How many questions in total does Amelia need to complete?

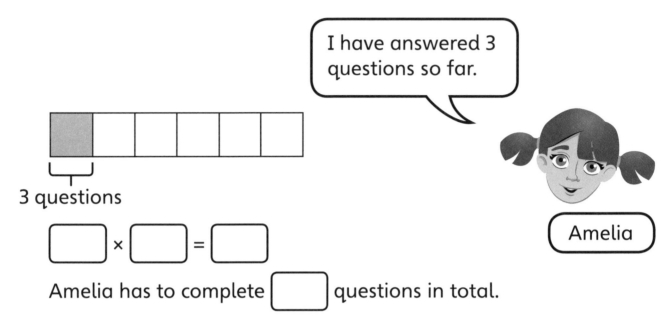

I have answered 3 questions so far.

Amelia

3 questions

▢ × ▢ = ▢

Amelia has to complete ▢ questions in total.

b) Amelia has learnt $\frac{2}{5}$ of her spellings homework.

How many spellings does she have to learn in total?

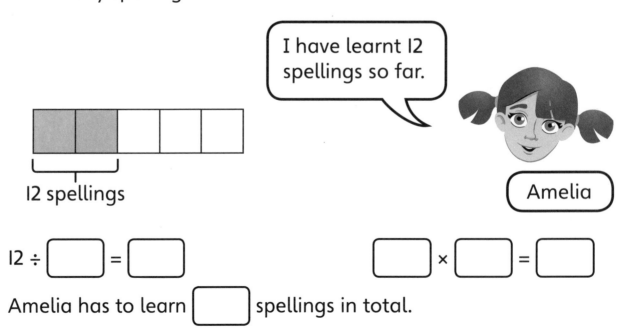

I have learnt 12 spellings so far.

Amelia

12 spellings

12 ÷ ▢ = ▢   ▢ × ▢ = ▢

Amelia has to learn ▢ spellings in total.

2 **a)** $\frac{3}{5}$ of a number is 15.

What is the number?

The number is ☐.

15

b) $\frac{4}{9}$ of a number is 48.

What is the number?

The number is ☐.

3 A box contains some buttons.

$\frac{1}{5}$ of the buttons are taken out.

There are 24 buttons left.

How many buttons were there at the start?

There were ☐ buttons at the start.

4 Ethan has some money.

He gives $\frac{5}{7}$ of the money to his friend.

He has £12 left.

How much money does he give to his friend?

Ethan gives £☐ to his friend.

5 Fill in the missing boxes.

a) $\dfrac{3}{5}$ of [ ] = 9

b) $\dfrac{\boxed{}}{9}$ of 27 = 12

CHALLENGE

6 Jen and Toshi are driving back from a holiday.

They are going to share the driving.

Jen is going to do $\dfrac{4}{9}$ of the driving.

Toshi knows he is going to drive for 40 km.

What is the total distance they have to drive?

The total distance Jen and Toshi have to drive is [ ] km.

Reflect

Draw a diagram to explain how you would work out the whole amount if $\dfrac{3}{5}$ is equal to £60.

Problem solving – fraction of a quantity ❷

1 Which is greater $\frac{1}{3}$ of 18, or $\frac{2}{9}$ of 36?

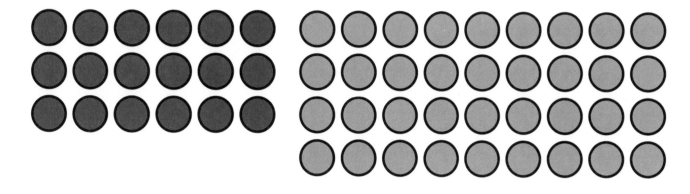

_____ is greater.

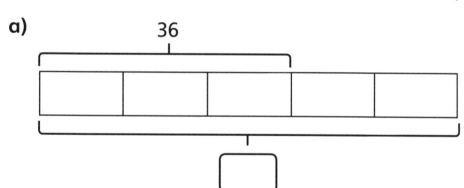

2 Work out the missing values in these fraction strips.

a)

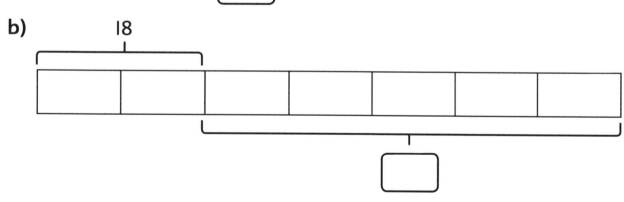

3 **a)** Mary has 16 cubes.

16 cubes

$\frac{1}{8}$ of the cubes are red.

$\frac{3}{8}$ of the cubes are blue.

The rest of the cubes are yellow.

How many of each colour cube are there?

Red = ☐   Blue = ☐   Yellow = ☐

b) Gino has 40 pencils.

$\frac{3}{5}$ of the pencils are red.

$\frac{3}{8}$ of the remaining pencils are blue.

The rest are green.

How many of each coloured pencil are there?

Red = ☐   Blue = ☐   Green = ☐

4 Cailyn uses 18 place value counters to make a number.

$\frac{1}{6}$ of the counters are 100s.

$\frac{4}{9}$ of the counters are 10s.

The rest of the counters are 1s.

What number has Cailyn made?

Cailyn has made the number $\boxed{}$.

5 Find the missing numbers.

CHALLENGE

a) $\frac{3}{5}$ of 40 = $\frac{2}{3}$ of $\boxed{}$

b) $\frac{3}{5}$ of 40 = $\dfrac{2}{\boxed{}}$ of 60

Reflect

$\frac{2}{3}$ of a number is 18.

Eva thinks that the number is 12 because 18 ÷ 3 = 6 and then 6 × 2 = 12.

Explain Eva's mistake.

→ Textbook 4B p160

End of unit check

My journal

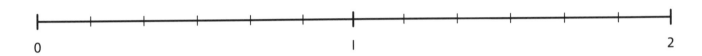

0   1   2

1 Explain the following equivalences. Use the number line to help you.

a) Explain why $1\frac{5}{6}$ is equal to $\frac{11}{6}$.

_____

_____

b) Explain why $\frac{5}{6} + \frac{3}{6}$ is equal to $1\frac{2}{6}$.

_____

_____

c) Explain why $2 - \frac{5}{6}$ is equal to $1\frac{1}{6}$.

_____

_____

Power check

How do you feel about your work in this unit?

Power puzzle

Holly is sharing some grapes with 4 children: Emma, Andy, Reena and Lee.

• Holly has 48 grapes.

• She gives $\frac{1}{6}$ of the grapes to Emma.

• She then eats 1 of the grapes that she has left.

• Holly then gives $\frac{1}{3}$ of the remaining grapes to Andy.

• Holly then eats 2 of the grapes she has left.

• She then gives $\frac{3}{8}$ of the remaining grapes to Reena.

• Holly then eats 3 of the grapes that are left.

• Holly finally gives Lee $\frac{3}{4}$ of the grapes she has remaining.

• Holly eats the grapes that she has left.

How many grapes does Holly eat in total?

Who gets the most grapes?

Create your own story like this and then swap with a partner.

→ Textbook 4B p164

Tenths

1 What numbers do the following representations show?

a)

$\frac{1}{10}$	$\frac{1}{10}$			

This shows $\frac{\boxed{}}{\boxed{}}$ or $\boxed{} . \boxed{}$.

b)

O	•	Tth
	•	0·1 0·1 0·1 0·1

This shows $\frac{\boxed{}}{\boxed{}}$ or $\boxed{} . \boxed{}$.

c)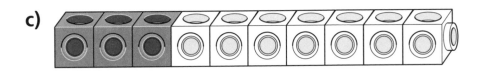

The white cubes represent $\frac{\boxed{}}{\boxed{}}$ or $\boxed{} . \boxed{}$.

The grey cubes represent $\frac{\boxed{}}{\boxed{}}$ or $\boxed{} . \boxed{}$.

d)

The white beads represent $\frac{\boxed{}}{\boxed{}}$ or $\boxed{} . \boxed{}$.

The grey beads represent $\frac{\boxed{}}{\boxed{}}$ or $\boxed{} . \boxed{}$.

2 Complete the models below to show each decimal number:

a) Draw counters to show 0·3.

T	O	•	Tth
		•	

b) The ten frame represents one whole. Draw enough counters to represent 0·8.

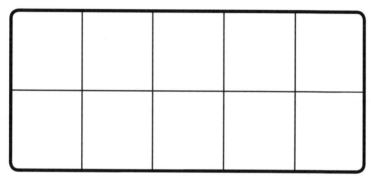

3 Complete the following number sentences.

a) $\frac{1}{10}$ = ☐ . ☐

b) 0·3 = ☐ / ☐

c) 0·7 = ☐ / ☐

d) $\frac{6}{10}$ = ☐ . ☐

4 Complete the missing numbers on the number line.

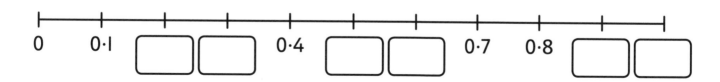

5 Emma has written the value of the place value counter as: 1·10.

Is she correct or incorrect? Explain your answer.

Emma is correct / incorrect because _____

_____ .

6 Alex thinks of a number.

CHALLENGE

- It is less than 1.
- It has an even digit in the tenths column.
- It can be made with more than 7 counters on a ten frame.

What number is she thinking of?

Alex is thinking of [ ]·[ ] .

How many different ways could you represent the number 0·6?

Tenths ②

1   Look at the representations below. Complete the sentences.

a)

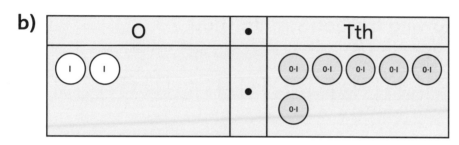

O	•	Tth
① ① ① ①	•	⓪·¹ ⓪·¹ ⓪·¹

The number ⬚ · ⬚ has ⬚ ones and ⬚ tenths.

b)

O	•	Tth
① ①	•	⓪·¹ ⓪·¹ ⓪·¹ ⓪·¹ ⓪·¹ ⓪·¹

The number ⬚ · ⬚ has ⬚ ones and ⬚ tenths.

c)

T	O	•	Tth
		•	

The number 40·6 has ⬚ tens, ⬚ ones and ⬚ tenths.

d)

T	O	•	Tth
		•	

The number ⬚ · ⬚ has 7 tens, 5 ones and 1 tenth.

2

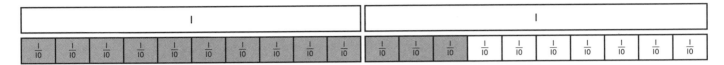

a) What number is shaded above?

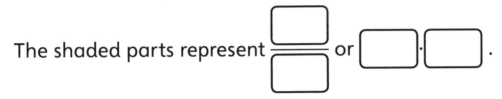

The shaded parts represent $\dfrac{\boxed{}}{\boxed{}}$ or $\boxed{} \cdot \boxed{}$.

b) Shade the following fraction strip to show 2·3.

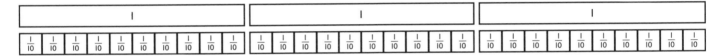

3 Match each statement to the correct number.

This number has 7 tenths.	74·5
The digit in the tenths column is I more than the digit in the ones column.	7·6
There are more ones than tenths.	0·7
This number has I5 tenths.	1·5

4 How can you write the number shown, as a decimal?

O	•	Tth
	•	0·1 0·1 0·1 0·1 0·1
	•	0·1 0·1 0·1 0·1 0·1

I will use a ten frame to help me see how to write this number.

The number shown is _____ .

5 Answer the following problems using the digit cards.

CHALLENGE

6	7	2	8

a) The largest number that can be made is ⬚·⬚ .

b) The smallest number that can be made is ⬚·⬚ .

c) 82 < ⬚⬚·⬚ < 83   82 < ⬚⬚·⬚ < 83

Reflect

Max says 12·3 has 1 in the tenths column. Is Max correct? What is the value of each of the digits?

_____

_____

_____

→ Textbook 4B p172

Tenths ❸

1   What is the length of each bug?

a)

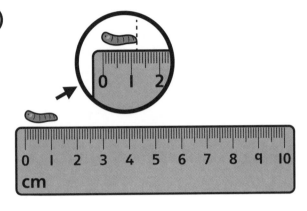

The worm is

☐.☐ cm long.

b)

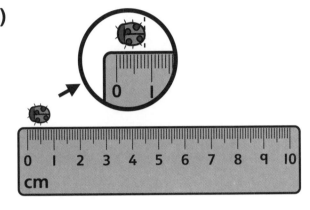

The ladybird is

☐.☐ cm long.

2   How much water is in each of the containers below?

a)

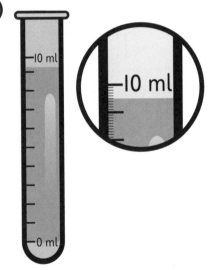

The container holds

☐.☐ ml of water.

b)

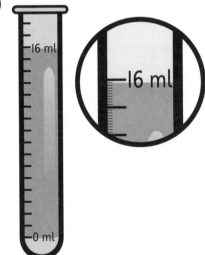

The container holds

☐.☐ ml of water.

3 **a)** How long is the grasshopper?

The grasshopper is ⬚ · ⬚ cm long.

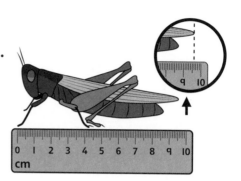

b) Another grasshopper is 0·7 cm shorter. How long is the second grasshopper?

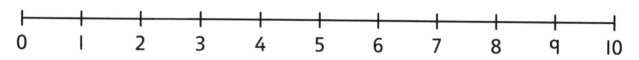

The second grasshopper is ⬚ · ⬚ cm long.

4 Complete the bottom scale to show the decimal equivalent of each fraction.

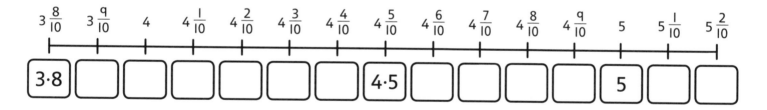

$3\frac{8}{10}$ $3\frac{9}{10}$ 4 $4\frac{1}{10}$ $4\frac{2}{10}$ $4\frac{3}{10}$ $4\frac{4}{10}$ $4\frac{5}{10}$ $4\frac{6}{10}$ $4\frac{7}{10}$ $4\frac{8}{10}$ $4\frac{9}{10}$ 5 $5\frac{1}{10}$ $5\frac{2}{10}$

3·8 ⬚ ⬚ ⬚ ⬚ ⬚ 4·5 ⬚ ⬚ ⬚ ⬚ 5 ⬚ ⬚

5 Record the position of the following numbers on the number line below.

3·9 $4\frac{1}{2}$ 4·6   5·0

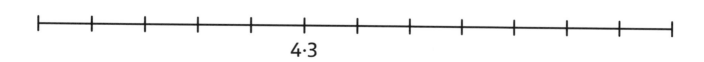

4·3

6 The number line below has not been labelled correctly.

Explain the mistake that has been made. Then rewrite the number line correctly.

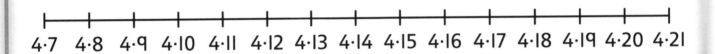

4·7 4·8 4·9 4·10 4·11 4·12 4·13 4·14 4·15 4·16 4·17 4·18 4·19 4·20 4·21

The mistake that has been made is _____

_____

_____

_____ .

Reflect

$5\frac{4}{10}$ is the same as 5·4.

Explain how you know if this is true.

Dividing by 10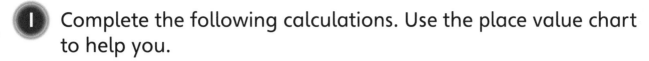

1 Complete the following calculations. Use the place value chart to help you.

a)

O	•	Tth
① ①	•	

O	•	Tth
	•	0·1 0·1 0·1 0·1 0·1 0·1 0·1 0·1 0·1 0·1 0·1 0·1 0·1 0·1 0·1 0·1 0·1 0·1 0·1 0·1

2 ones = ☐ tenths

☐ tenths ÷ 10 = ☐ tenths

2 ÷ 10 = ☐ . ☐

b)

O	•	Tth
① ① ① ① ① ① ① ①	•	

8 ones = ☐ tenths

☐ tenths ÷ 10 = ☐ tenths

So 8 ÷ 10 = ☐ . ☐

c)

O	•	Tth
① ① ① ① ① ① ①	•	

7 ÷ 10 = ☐ . ☐

129

2 Complete the following bar model and record the calculation that it represents.

5									

$$\boxed{} \div \boxed{} = \boxed{}$$

3 Max says, 'I divided by 10 is equal to 10 tenths.'

O	•	Tth		O	•	Tth
①						0·1 0·1 0·1 0·1 0·1
	•				•	0·1 0·1 0·1 0·1 0·1

Explain Max's mistake and give the correct answer.

_____

_____

4 Complete the following calculations.

a) $6 \div 10 = 0{\cdot}\boxed{}$

b) $8 \div \boxed{} = 0{\cdot}8$

c) $1 \div 10 = \boxed{}$

d) $0 \div 10 = \boxed{}$

e) $\boxed{} \div 10 = 0{\cdot}4$

f) $0{\cdot}5 = \boxed{} \div 10$

g) $0{\cdot}3 = 3 \div \boxed{}$

h) $\boxed{} \div 10 = 1$

5 Do you agree or disagree with the following calculation?

$$5 \div 10 = 2$$

I agree / disagree because _____

_____

_____ .

6 What patterns can you spot in the following calculations?

$1 \div 10 = 0 \cdot 1$

$2 \div 10 = 0 \cdot 2$

$3 \div 10 = 0 \cdot 3$

I notice that _____

_____

_____ .

Reflect

Explain how to divide a 1-digit number by 10.

131

→ Textbook 4B p180

Dividing by 10 ❷

1 Complete the following calculations.

a) 2 tens = [ ] ones

[ ] ones ÷ 10 = [ ] ones

4 ones = [ ] tenths

[ ] tenths ÷ 10 = [ ] tenths

So, 24 ÷ 10 = [ ] ones and

[ ] tenths = [ ].[ ]

T	O	•	Tth
⑩⑩	①①①①	•	

T	O	•	Tth
	①①①①① ①①①①① ①①①①① ①①①①①	•	⑴⑴⑴⑴⑴ ⑴⑴⑴⑴⑴ ⑴⑴⑴⑴⑴ ⑴⑴⑴⑴⑴ ⑴⑴⑴⑴⑴ ⑴⑴⑴⑴⑴ ⑴⑴⑴⑴⑴ ⑴⑴⑴⑴⑴

b) 4 tens = [ ] ones

[ ] ones ÷ 10 = [ ] ones

5 ones = [ ] tenths

[ ] tenths ÷ 10 = [ ] tenths

So, 45 ÷ 10 = [ ] ones and [ ] tenths = [ ].[ ]

T	O	•	Tth
⑩⑩⑩⑩	①①①①①	•	

c) 51 ÷ 10 = [ ]

T	O	•	Tth
⑩⑩⑩⑩⑩	①	•	

2 Complete the bar model and the calculation it represents.

28

$\boxed{} \div \boxed{} = \boxed{}$

3 Describe what happens to each digit when you divide 47 by 10.

T	O	•	Tth
		•	

_____

_____

_____

4 Are the following calculations true or false? Circle your answer.

$43 \div 10 = 3 \cdot 4$ True / False

$10 \div 43 = 4 \cdot 3$ True / False

$43 \div 10 = 4 \cdot 3$ True / False

$4 \cdot 3 = 43 \div 10$ True / False

5 Complete the following calculations.

a) $46 \div 10 = \boxed{}$

d) $\boxed{} = 39 \div 10$

b) $\boxed{} \div 10 = 1 \cdot 8$

e) $\boxed{} \div 10 = 3 \cdot 9$

c) $\boxed{} \div 10 = 7 \cdot 2$

f) $6 \cdot 5 = \boxed{} \div 10$

6 Is the following statement always, sometimes or never true? Provide examples to support your answer.

'A 2-digit number divided by 10 will always have an answer with a digit in the tenths column.'

Always true   Sometimes true   Never true

7 How many different ways is it possible to complete the following using a 2-digit number?

CHALLENGE

$$7 \cdot 9 > \boxed{} \div 10 > 7 \cdot 3$$

☐ ways.

Reflect

What is the same and what is different about dividing a 1-digit number by 10 and dividing a 2-digit number by 10?

Hundredths

1. Complete the following so that the hundredths grid, fraction and decimal in each part are equivalent to each other.

a)

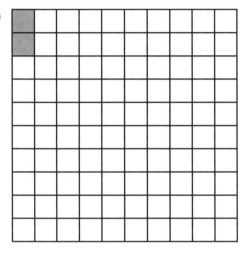

$$\frac{\boxed{}}{100}$$

$\boxed{}\,.\,\boxed{}\,\boxed{}$

b)

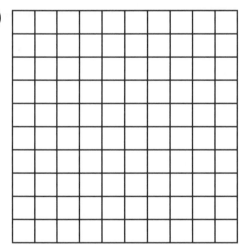

$$\frac{14}{100}$$

$\boxed{}\,.\,\boxed{}\,\boxed{}$

c)

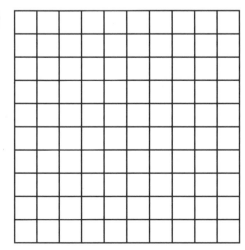

$$\frac{\boxed{}}{\boxed{}}$$

$0{\cdot}05$

2 How could the following be written as a fraction and as a decimal?

$$\frac{\boxed{}}{\boxed{}} \text{ or } \boxed{} \cdot \boxed{}$$

3 Complete the table.

Fraction:	$\frac{16}{100}$	$\frac{18}{100}$		$\frac{22}{100}$	
Decimal:	0·16		0·20		

4 Complete these equivalent fractions and decimals.

a) $\frac{32}{100} = 0\cdot\boxed{}$

b) $0\cdot27 = \frac{\boxed{}}{100}$

c) $0\cdot39 = \frac{\boxed{}}{\boxed{}}$

d) Nineteen hundredths

$= \boxed{} \cdot \boxed{}$

e) $0\cdot46 = \boxed{}$ hundredths

f) $\frac{\boxed{}}{100} = 0\cdot52$

g) $0\cdot59 = \frac{\boxed{}}{\boxed{}}$

h) $\frac{\boxed{}}{\boxed{}} = 0\cdot93$

i) Ninety hundredths

$= \boxed{} \cdot \boxed{}$

j) $0\cdot03 = \boxed{}$ hundredths

5 Jamie says 0·2 of the grid is shaded.

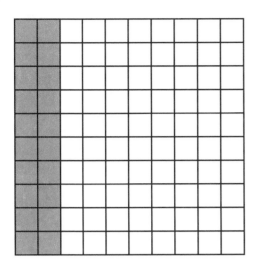

There are more than 2 squares shaded on the hundredths grid, so I wonder if Jamie is correct.

Do you agree or disagree with Jamie? Explain your answer.

_____

_____

_____

Reflect

$0·07 = \frac{7}{100}$

Explain how you know that this calculation is true.

_____

_____

_____

137

→ Textbook 4B p188

Hundredths ❷

1 Complete these questions so that the diagram, fraction and decimal in each part are all equivalent.

a)

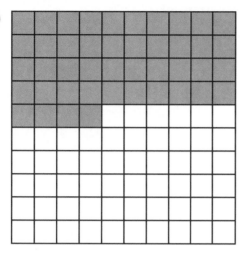

$\dfrac{\boxed{}}{100}$

$\boxed{} . \boxed{}$

b)

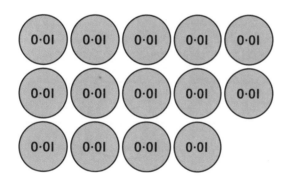

$\dfrac{\boxed{}}{100}$

$\boxed{} . \boxed{}$

c)

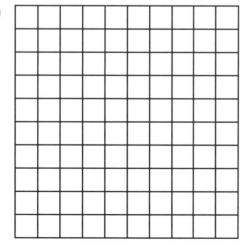

$\dfrac{\boxed{}}{\boxed{}}$

0·15

2 Mo, Isla and Zac have shared 100 counters between them.

Use the bar model to calculate what fraction of the whole each child has. Record this as a decimal.

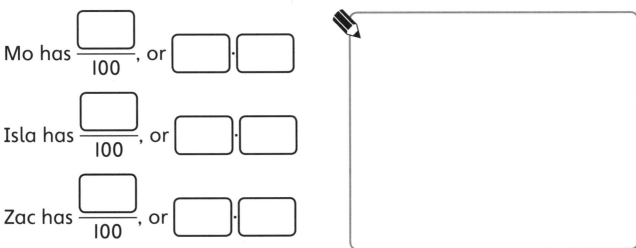

100		
Isla 45	Mo 23	Zac ?

Mo has $\dfrac{\boxed{}}{100}$, or $\boxed{}.\boxed{}$

Isla has $\dfrac{\boxed{}}{100}$, or $\boxed{}.\boxed{}$

Zac has $\dfrac{\boxed{}}{100}$, or $\boxed{}.\boxed{}$

3 Use the digits 0 and 5 to complete the calculation below.
Each digit can be used more than once.

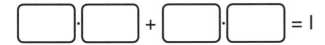

$\boxed{}.\boxed{} + \boxed{}.\boxed{} = 1$

4 Emma has 100 cards. She loses 17 of them. What fraction of the cards does she have left? Give your answer as a decimal too.

$\dfrac{\boxed{}}{\boxed{}}$ $\boxed{}.\boxed{}$

5 Luis writes the number of shaded squares as 0·5 of the hundredths grid.

Do you agree or disagree with Luis?

I agree / disagree because _____

_____

_____ .

6 Ebo has been asked to show 0·40 on a hundredths grid.

CHALLENGE

He doesn't think this is possible as he thinks there are 0 hundredths in 0·40.

What advice would you give Ebo to help him to understand that it is possible to show 0·40 on a hundredths grid.

_____

_____

_____

Reflect

How many different ways can the following be completed?

$0.3 < \boxed{} < 0.4$

_____

_____

_____

Hundredths ③

Remember that 10 hundredths are equal to 1 tenth.

1 Complete the sentences.

a)

O	•	Tth	Hth
	•	0·1 0·1 0·1	0·01 0·01 0·01 0·01 0·01

The ☐ tenth counters represent 0·3.

The ☐ hundredth counters represent 0·05.

☐ tenths and ☐ hundredths make 0·☐ .

b)

O	•	Tth	Hth
	•	0·1 0·1 0·1 0·1 0·1	0·01 0·01 0·01

The ☐ tenth counters represent ☐ .

The ☐ hundredth counters represent ☐ .

☐ tenths and ☐ hundredths make 0·☐ .

c)

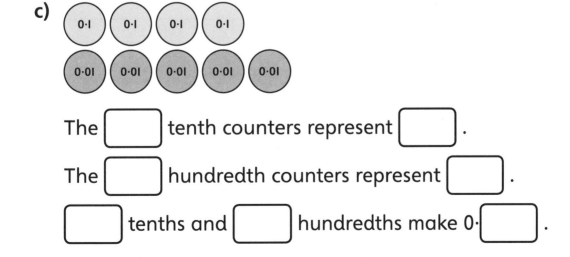

The ☐ tenth counters represent ☐ .

The ☐ hundredth counters represent ☐ .

☐ tenths and ☐ hundredths make 0·☐ .

2 Complete the following part-whole models.

a)

0·67
0·6 ◯

c)

0·87
◯ 0·07

b)

0·82
0·02 ◯

d)

◯
0·7 0·05

3 Complete the following expressions.

a) 0·37 = 3 tenths and ☐ hundredths

b) 0·37 = 2 tenths and ☐ hundredths

c) 0·37 = I tenth and ☐ hundredths

d) 0·37 = ☐ hundredths

O	•	Tth	Hth
	•	0·1 0·1 0·1	0·01 0·01 0·01 0·01 0·01 0·01 0·01

4 Complete the following.

a) 0·47 = 0·☐ and 0·☐

b) 0·3 and 0·05 = ☐·☐

c) 0·4 and ☐·☐ = 0·☐6

d) 0·51 = 0·☐ and 0·☐

e) 0·09 and 0·3 = ☐·☐

f) 0·3☐ = 0·☐ and 0·07

5 Luis has the following place value counters.

(0·01) (0·01) (0·01) (0·01) (0·01) (0·01) (0·1) (0·1) (0·1)

He writes the number as 0·63.

Do you agree or disagree with Luis? Explain your answer.

_____

_____

6 Lee has the following place value counters. He adds them to a place value grid one by one. What number is represented after each counter is added?

CHALLENGE

(0·1) (0·1) (0·1) (0·01) (0·01) (0·1) (0·01) (0·01) (0·01) (0·01) (0·01) (0·01) (0·1) (0·01) (0·01)

_____

_____

Reflect

Explain how 57 hundredths can be made up of tenths and hundredths. How many different ways can you find to do it?

_____

_____

_____

_____

→ Textbook 4B p196

Dividing by 100

 1 Complete the following calculations.

a) $5 \div 100$

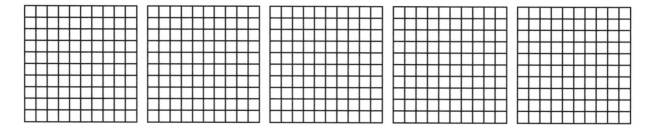

5 ones = ☐ hundredths

☐ hundredths $\div$ 100 = ☐ hundredths

So, $5 \div 100 =$ ☐ . ☐

b) $11 \div 100$

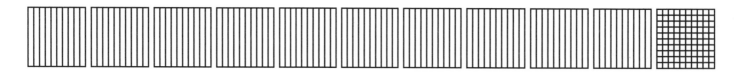

10 squares split into 10 parts means there are ☐ tenths.

☐ tenths $\div$ 100 = ☐ tenth(s)

1 square split into 100 pieces means there are ☐ hundredths.

☐ hundredths $\div$ 100 = ☐ hundredth(s)

$11 \div 100 =$ ☐ . ☐

2 Aki is dividing 15 by 100.

I have noticed that when you divide by 100 the digits move columns.

T	O	•	Tth	Hth
1	5	•		

Explain what happens to the digits when you divide by 100.

_____

_____

3 Complete the calculations using the examples in **bold** to help you.

7 ÷ 100 = 0·07   **13 ÷ 100 = 0·13**   **45 ÷ 100 = 0·45**

a) 8 ÷ 100 = ▢   c) 14 ÷ 100 = ▢   e) 55 ÷ 100 = ▢

b) 9 ÷ 100 = ▢   d) 15 ÷ 100 = ▢   f) 65 ÷ 100 = ▢

4 Are the following statements true or false? Write your answer in the table.

When you divide by 100:

	True or False?
The digits change.	
Any digit in the ones column moves to the tenths column.	
Any digit in the tens column moves to the tenths column.	
Each digit becomes $\frac{1}{100}$ of the value.	

5 Complete the following calculations.

a) $54 \div 100 =$ ☐

e) $35 \div 100 =$ ☐

b) ☐ $\div 100 = 0.63$

f) ☐ $\div 100 = 0.36$

c) $0.05 =$ ☐ $\div 100$

g) $0.5 =$ ☐ $\div 100$

d) ☐ $= 32 \div 100$

h) ☐ $= 23 \div 100$

6 a) If I divide 45 by 100, what will the value of the digit 5 be in the answer?

CHALLENGE

The value of the digit 5 in the answer is _____ .

b) If I find $\frac{1}{100}$ of 59, what will the value of the digit 9 be in the answer?

The value of the digit 9 in the answer is _____ .

Reflect

Explain how knowing $\frac{12}{100} = 0.12$ helps you work out $12 \div 100$.

_____

_____

_____

Dividing by 10 and 100

1 **a)** There are 10 boxes of plates.

The total mass of the boxes is 45 kg.

What is the mass of each box?

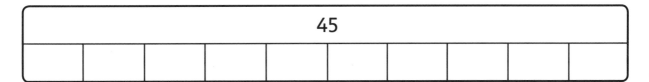

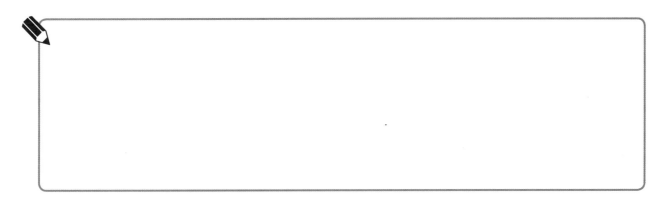

The mass of each box is [　　] kg.

b) Bowls come in boxes of 10.

The mass of 10 boxes is 30 kg.

What is the mass of each bowl?

The mass of each bowl is [　　] kg.

2 What calculation does the bar model represent?

83								
8·3								

$$\boxed{} \div \boxed{} = \boxed{}$$

3 Circle the value of the underlined digit in 12·1<u>3</u>.

3 hundreds   3 tenths   3 ones   3 hundredths

4 Complete the following calculations.

a) $56 \div 10 = \boxed{}\cdot\boxed{}$

   $56 \div 100 = \boxed{}\cdot\boxed{}$

b) $\boxed{} \div 10 = 3\cdot4$

   $\boxed{} \div 100 = 0\cdot34$

c) $72 \div 10 = \boxed{}\cdot\boxed{}$

   $72 \div 100 = 0\cdot\boxed{}$

d) $14 \div \boxed{} = 1\cdot4$

   $14 \div \boxed{} = 0\cdot14$

5 Complete the following equations.

a) $68 \div 10 = \boxed{}\cdot\boxed{}$

b) $46 \div 100 = \boxed{}\cdot\boxed{}$

c) $\boxed{}\cdot\boxed{} = 18 \div 100$

d) $4\cdot9 = 49 \div \boxed{}$

e) $0\cdot97 = \boxed{} \div 100$

f) $0 \div 100 = \boxed{}$

6 **a)** Danny divides a number by 10 and he gets 9·6.

What would he get if he divided his number by 100?

Explain your working.

_____

_____

b) Bella divides a number by 100 and gets 0·07. What does Bella get if she divides her number by 10?

Explain your working.

_____

_____

7 Prove that $\frac{1}{10}$ of 7 is equal to $\frac{1}{100}$ of 70. Show your working.

Reflect

Explain the link between dividing a number by 10 and dividing the same number by 100.

→ Textbook 4B p204

End of unit check

My journal

1   How many different numbers can you make using the digit cards
    below? You must use all the cards in each number you make.

2   Choose one of the numbers you have made and represent it in as many
    different visual ways as possible. What is the value of these digits?

Power check

How do you feel about your work in this unit?

Power play

- In pairs, use a spinner, like the one shown, to make a journey through the grid.

- If you move off the grid (for example, if you spin 0·1 less or 0·01 less on your first go), then you move back to (or stay on) 0·01 and it is your partner's turn.

- Who can get the furthest after 12 goes?

0·01	0·02	0·03	0·04	0·05	0·06	0·07	0·08	0·09	0·10
0·11	0·12	0·13	0·14	0·15	0·16	0·17	0·18	0·19	0·20
0·21	0·22	0·23	0·24	0·25	0·26	0·27	0·28	0·29	0·30
0·31	0·32	0·33	0·34	0·35	0·36	0·37	0·38	0·39	0·40
0·41	0·42	0·43	0·44	0·45	0·46	0·47	0·48	0·49	0·50
0·51	0·52	0·53	0·54	0·55	0·56	0·57	0·58	0·59	0·60
0·61	0·62	0·63	0·64	0·65	0·66	0·67	0·68	0·69	0·70
0·71	0·72	0·73	0·74	0·75	0·76	0·77	0·78	0·79	0·80
0·81	0·82	0·83	0·84	0·85	0·86	0·87	0·88	0·89	0·90
0·91	0·92	0·93	0·94	0·95	0·96	0·97	0·98	0·99	1·00

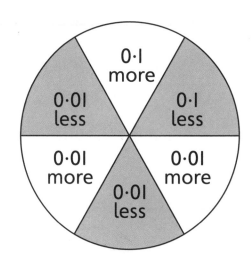

Here is an example:

- Player 1 starts on 0·01.

- On their first go, player 1 spins 0·01 more, so they count on 1 hundredth and move to 0·02.

- On their second go, player 1 spins 0·1 more, so moves from 0·02 to 0·12.

My power points

Colour in the ☆ to show what you have learnt.

Colour in the ☺ if you feel happy about what you have learnt.

Unit 6

I can ...

☆ ☺ Solve problems using addition and multiplication

☆ ☺ Use the written column method to multiply

☆ ☺ Multiply a 2-digit number by a 1-digit number

☆ ☺ Multiply a 3-digit number by a 1-digit number

☆ ☺ Multiply more than two numbers

☆ ☺ Divide a 2-digit number by a 1-digit number

☆ ☺ Divide with remainders

☆ ☺ Divide a 3-digit number by a 1-digit number

☆ ☺ Solve problems using division

Unit 7

I can ...

☆ ☺ Explain what area is

☆ ☺ Count squares to measure the area

☆ ☺ Make rectilinear shapes using squares

☆ ☺ Compare the areas of two shapes

Unit 8

I can …

☆ ☺ Use a hundredths grid to identify tenths and hundredths

☆ ☺ Write tenths and hundredths as fractions

☆ ☺ Use a fraction wall to show equivalent fractions

☆ ☺ Simplify fractions

☆ ☺ Recognise and show fractions greater than 1

Unit 9

I can …

☆ ☺ Add two or more fractions

☆ ☺ Subtract two fractions

☆ ☺ Subtract a fraction from a whole amount

☆ ☺ Solve problems by adding and subtracting fractions

☆ ☺ Solve word problems by adding and subtracting fractions

☆ ☺ Calculate fractions of a quantity

Unit 10

I can …

☆ ☺ Show tenths as a decimal

☆ ☺ Show tenths on a place value grid

☆ ☺ Represent tenths on a number line

☆ ☺ Divide a 1-digit number by 10

☆ ☺ Divide a 2-digit number by 10

☆ ☺ Show hundredths as a decimal

☆ ☺ Show hundredths on a place value grid

☆ ☺ Divide 1 and 2-digit numbers by 100

☆ ☺ Solve problems by dividing by 10 and 100

Keep up the good work!

153

Notes

Notes

Squared paper

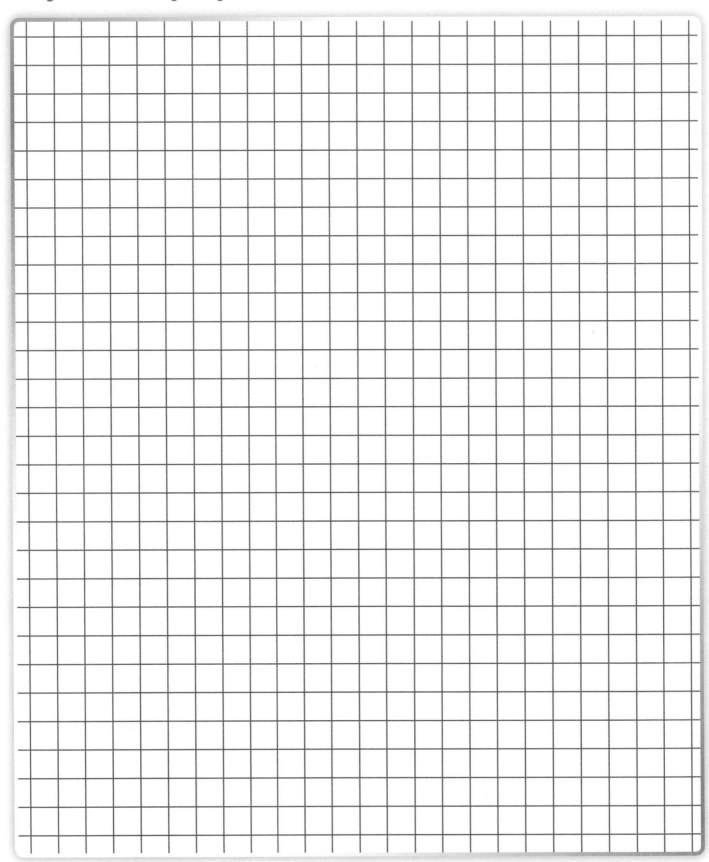

Squared paper

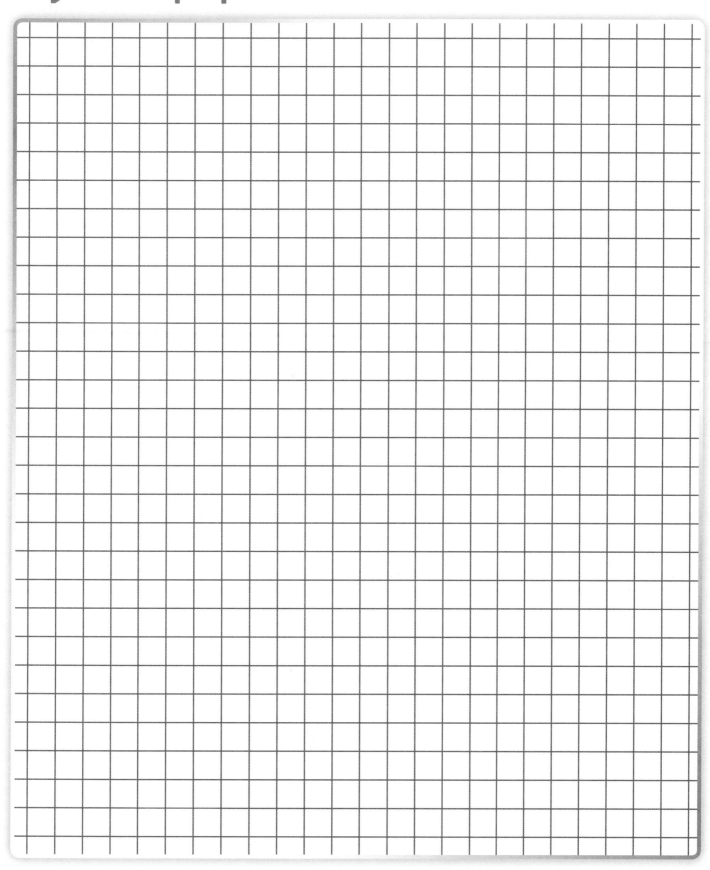

Squared paper

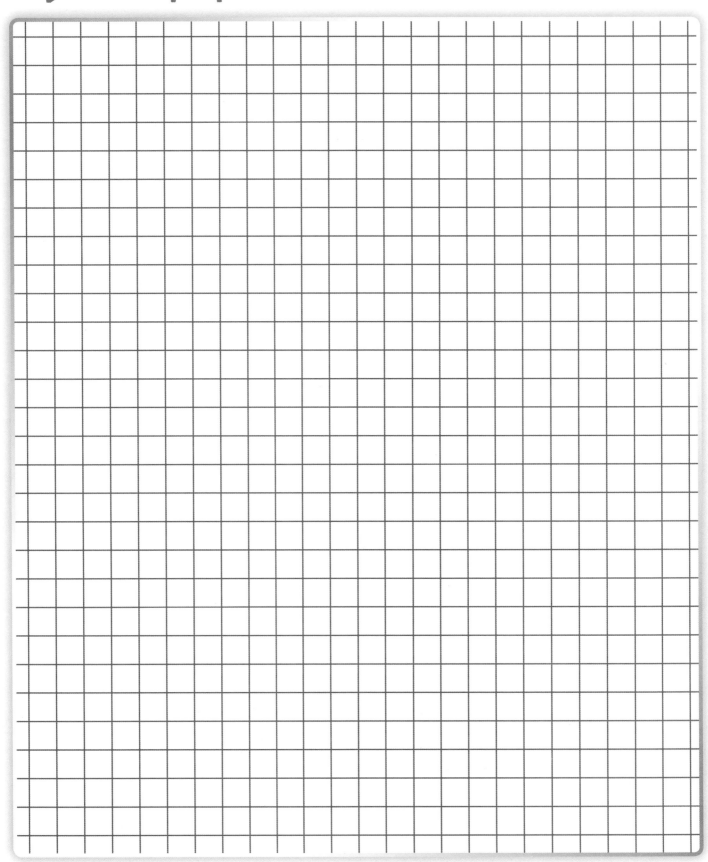

Squared paper

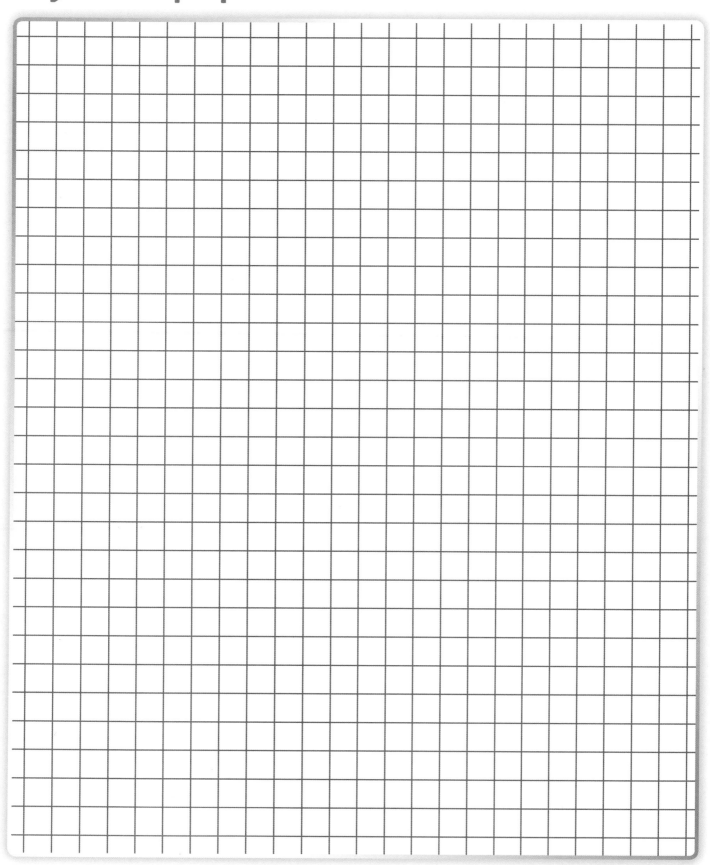

Squared paper

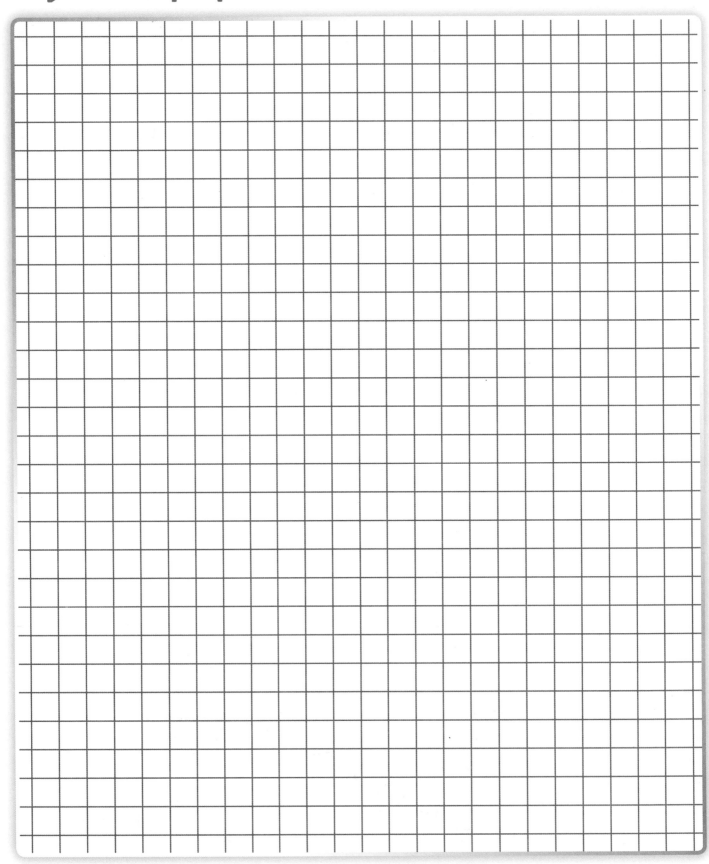